"Reading this book felt like compressing decades of billionaire investment wisdom into an afternoon. Bob and Ben simplify complex strategies in a way that reshapes how you think about risk, reward, and diversification. Whether you're just starting out or a seasoned investor, this book delivers clarity, depth, and a serious edge."

 —**JUSTIN DONALD,** #1 *WSJ* and *USA Today* bestselling author, founder of The Lifestyle Investor, and host of *The Lifestyle Investor* podcast

"You don't have to be a billionaire to invest like one! Now you can build your personal wealth with the secret strategies used by billionaires. *Invest Like a Billionaire* will not only change how you invest—it will elevate how you think."

 —**JON GORDON,** seventeen-time bestselling author of *The Energy Bus* and *The Power of Positive Leadership*

"Bob and Ben have written the rare kind of book that combines financial intelligence with moral clarity. *Invest Like a Billionaire* is essential for anyone serious about building wealth for greater impact."

 —**JOE JOHNSON,** CEO and founder of Life Surge

"*Invest Like a Billionaire*, by Bob and Ben Fraser, is a must-read for every investor. With decades of experience in finance at major global firms, I have read countless complex texts on modern portfolio theory and alternative investments. This book stands out for its clarity, breaking down complex concepts into simple, actionable terms accessible to all investors. Whether you're new to investing or refining your strategy, this book offers invaluable insights."

 —**ANTON MATTLI,** cofounder and CEO of Peak Financing

"In my thirty years advising high-net-worth clients, I've never seen a book that captures the essence of billionaire investing so clearly. *Invest Like a Billionaire* is not just a theoretical guide; it's a practical roadmap for success."

 —**JIM DEW,** CFP®, ChFC®, CPWA®, cofounder and CEO of Dew Wealth Management and the Fractional Family Office®

"So many successful people think investing is only stocks or bonds. There is a better way, and Bob and Ben take you behind the curtain of high-net-worth investment strategies. This is elite knowledge made accessible."
—**SEAN KOUPLEN,** chairman and CEO of Regent Bank

"I've followed Bob's macro insights for years—this book puts his proven strategy into a readable, repeatable playbook. If you want to be an informed investor with a cheat code to real wealth, read on."
—**JOEY MURE,** founder of Wealth Without Wall Street

"Bob and Ben are geniuses. This book is like having a private consultation with two brilliant investment minds—without the six-figure fee."
—**GRAHAM COCHRANE,** *USA Today* bestselling author of *Rebel* and *How to Get Paid for What You Know*

"Bob cuts through the noise with truth and clarity, showing families how to build lasting wealth with lower risk and greater peace."
—**DAVID BULL,** founder and CEO of Ark Financial

"The Frasers' ability to distill complex macro trends into simple, actionable insights is unparalleled. Their ability to find, analyze, and execute profitable alternative investments in profitable niches over multiple market cycles is impressive."
—**JACK KRUPEY,** fund manager

"To invest like a billionaire might seem impossible or counterintuitive for the average investor, but it is within any investor's reach when you take Bob and Ben's insights and put them into action."
—**PARKER WEBB,** CEO of BrightStar Property Group

"Bob's insights into investments and portfolio management offered a refreshing departure from traditional retail theories. He has been an invaluable source of knowledge."
—**S. ROSAS,** alternative investment analyst

"If you're tired of Wall Street volatility, this book is the calm in the storm."
—Joe Barton, founder and CEO of Barton Publishing

"*Invest Like a Billionaire* is clear, concise, and incredibly actionable."
> **—JASON WILSON,** founder and CEO of T&C Construction

"Bob's track record speaks volumes, and this book captures the strategy behind the success. It's practical, powerful, and well-timed."
> **—NOAH CUTLER,** managing director at North Fork Partners

"This book distills decades of real-world investing into strategies anyone can use. The clarity is rare—and that's what makes it powerful."
> **—ERIK VAN HORN,** cofounder of Front Street Equity Partners

"I'll be buying this book and sharing it with friends and clients. An excellent primer on the pathway to modern wealth creation."
> **—KENDALL LAUGHLIN,** family office director and executive coach at Ark Financial

"I've read a dozen investment books in the past year. This is the only one that stuck."
> **—LITAN YAHAV,** cofounder and CEO of Vyzer

"It's rare to find an investing book that's both backed by rigorous data and easy to read with clear, actionable steps. If you're ready to stop outsourcing control of your wealth and want proven frameworks for investing beyond the stock market, this is a must-read."
> **—CALEB GUILLIAMS,** founder of BetterWealth.com

"In *Invest Like a Billionaire*, Bob and Ben Fraser bring the data and the economic reasoning, making it clear why the ultra-wealthy are heavily invested in Alts. But even more importantly, they provide a compelling invitation and realistic access for anyone to enter the wonderful world of private investments."
> **—JIM MAFFUCCIO,** cofounder and managing director of Aspen Funds

INVEST
LIKE A
BILLIONAIRE

**UNLOCKING
THE WEALTH SECRETS
OF THE ULTRA-RICH**

BOB FRASER & BEN FRASER

Invest Like a Billionaire: Unlocking the Wealth Secrets of the Ultra-rich

Copyright © 2025 by Bob Fraser and Ben Fraser

All rights reserved. No part of this publication may be reproduced, stored in a retrieval system, or transmitted in any form by any means, electronic, mechanical, photocopy, recording, or otherwise, without the prior permission of the publisher, except as provided by USA copyright law.

No patent liability is assumed with respect to the use of the information contained herein. Although every precaution has been taken in the preparation of this book, the publisher and author assume no responsibility for errors or omissions. Neither is any liability assumed for damages resulting from the use of the information contained herein.

This book is intended for informational purposes only. It is not intended to be used as the sole basis for financial or investing decisions, nor should it be construed as advice designed to meet the particular needs of an individual's situation.

Published by Maxwell Leadership Publishing, an imprint of Forefront Books, Nashville, Tennessee.

Distributed by Simon & Schuster.

Scripture quotations are taken from the *Holy Bible*, New Living Translation, Copyright © 1996, 2004, 2015 by Tyndale House Foundation. Used by permission of Tyndale House Publishers, Inc., Carol Stream, Illinois 60188. All rights reserved.

A note to the reader: Plural pronouns throughout this book (we, us, etc.) refer to both authors. Where singular pronouns appear (I, me, my), that voice is predominantly Bob's.

Library of Congress Control Number: 2025911608

Print ISBN: 979-8-88710-052-4
E-book ISBN: 979-8-88710-053-1

Cover Design by Bruce Gore, Gore Studio, Inc.
Interior Design by Bill Kersey, KerseyGraphics

Printed in the United States of America

25 26 27 28 29 30 [LAK] 10 9 8 7 6 5 4 3 2 1

DEDICATION

This is dedicated to my three partners at Aspen Funds: Jim Maffuccio, Dan Schulte, and Ben Fraser, who have made the ride a joy.
– Bob Fraser

To Laura, my bride and companion. Thank you for your unwavering support and belief in me. Life is way more fun with you.
– Ben Fraser

CONTENTS

Foreword 11
Introduction 13

PART 1
THE BILLIONAIRE FACTOR

Chapter 1: The Billionaire Investor 19
Chapter 2: What Makes Billionaires Different from You and Me 29
Chapter 3: 7 Things Your Financial Advisor Will Never Tell You 39
Chapter 4: What Billionaires Know About the Stock Market 47
Chapter 5: What Makes Private Alts So Attractive 65

PART 2
DEEP DIVE: PRIVATE ALTS

Chapter 6: Private Real Estate 93
Chapter 7: Private Credit 119
Chapter 8: Private Equity 131
Chapter 9: Venture Capital 139
Chapter 10: Hedge Funds 145
Chapter 11: Oil & Gas, Gold, Crypto, and MORE 155
Chapter 12: Stocks and Bonds 173

PART 3
ALTS HOW-TO GUIDE

Chapter 13: How Billionaires Beat the Tax Man 183

Chapter 14: Organizing and Structuring Your Investments 203

Chapter 15: Building a Smart Portfolio 213

Chapter 16: How to Select an Operator. 223

Chapter 17: How to Spot the Losers. 233

Chapter 18: Navigate a PPM In thirty Minutes 245

Chapter 19: Decoding the Numbers 257

Conclusion 277

Appendix A: If You're Not Accredited. 279

Appendix B: Fat Tails 289

Acknowledgments 293

Notes 291

About the Authors. 299

Invest Like a Billionaire **Podcast** 301

About Aspen Funds 303

FOREWORD

Great leaders don't leave their future to chance—they shape it with the choices they make every day. The same is true for financial success. Whether you realize it or not, the decisions you make about money today will determine your financial future tomorrow.

This lesson is personal to me. My brother, Larry, is an incredibly successful businessman and investor. Over the years, I've watched him make calculated, disciplined decisions that allowed him to build lasting wealth. But what's most fascinating isn't just what he invested in—it's how he thought about money.

Larry never chased quick wins or followed the crowd. Instead, he thought long-term, prioritized fundamentals, and made decisions based on principles, not emotions. He approached investing the same way great leaders approach their organizations—with vision, strategy, and patience.

Larry's financial wisdom made a tangible impact on my own life. In my early years, as I was just getting started in my career, it was Larry's financial success that helped launch me. His generosity and belief in my leadership journey were only possible because he had built a strong financial foundation. That experience taught me something profound: Financial success isn't just about wealth—it's about the freedom to impact others.

Over the years, I've had the privilege of getting to know Bob Fraser through our shared passion for values-based global transformation. It's clear that Bob approaches investing with the same principles I believe make great leaders—discipline, vision, and stewardship. His ability to break down how the most successful investors think and act is what makes *Invest Like a Billionaire* such a valuable resource.

Successful investors don't panic when markets dip or get caught up in hype when prices soar. They don't let fear or excitement dictate their financial future. Instead, they follow proven principles, looking beyond the noise to see the bigger picture.

They also embody the timeless leadership principles that drive long-term success:

- Vision – The best leaders don't just see what's happening today; they see more. This book will help you see more about how the most successful investors invest—so you can apply the same strategies to your own financial future.
- Discipline – They stick to their principles and investment strategies, even when emotions or external pressures tempt them to do otherwise.
- They think in decades, not days. Instead of chasing short-term trends, they position themselves to create generational wealth.
- They invest in opportunities others overlook. When most people follow the crowd, the most successful investors look where no one else is looking.

The insights in *Invest Like a Billionaire* will give you the tools to make smarter financial choices and take control of your financial future. As you turn these pages, approach them not just as an investor, but as a leader—because the way you manage your money is a reflection of how you lead your life.

Your financial future is determined by the decisions you make today. Make them wisely.

Your friend,

John C. Maxwell

#1 *New York Time* bestselling author, founder of Maxwell Leadership

INTRODUCTION

This book might be one of the most important you will ever read.

Behind your health and your relationships, your financial well-being is probably the most important thing that will determine your future.

And because of the laws of compounding, over the long haul, your investment choices *will* determine your financial future, even more than your career choices.

That is why the ultrawealthy spend so much time on their investment, allowing them to consistently earn higher returns with less risk and lower volatility. In this book, we will unlock the power of private alternatives, the very investment vehicles that form the foundation of their success, which were previously locked away from smaller investors until a landmark regulation change in 2012.

However, as you will learn, the financial system is still not geared to help you invest in these powerful vehicles, and a certain amount of expertise is required to successfully access them.

Hence this book.

We will give you all the tools you need to understand and break into this not-so-mysterious world—and do so successfully.

ACCREDITED INVESTORS

This book is written primarily to accredited investors—those who, according to Securities and Exchange Commission (SEC) rules, are permitted to invest in private placements. Accredited investors are those who (1) have at least a $1 million net worth, excluding their primary residence, or (2) have earned $200,000 (or $300,000 jointly with their spouse) in income in the last two years, with the expectation of doing the same this year. There are several other categories, but these are the ones that apply to most folks.

That said, if you are not yet accredited, don't be discouraged—you still have a lot of options. We outline them in Appendix A: *If You're Not Accredited*. So keep reading this book; you can use most of our techniques and strategies even while you work toward becoming accredited.

Let's dive in and see just what billionaires know that you probably don't.

PART 1

THE BILLIONAIRE FACTOR

CHAPTER 1

THE BILLIONAIRE INVESTOR

*"An investment in **knowledge** pays the best interest."*
- Benjamin Franklin

David's mother was a Lutheran minister and his father a university professor in small-town Wisconsin. The first sign something was different about David was in the third grade, when his teachers came to his parents and said, "We need David to skip this grade. He's just way ahead, and we have to put a special teacher with him all the time."

David Swensen went on to earn a PhD in economics from Yale, then took a stint on Wall Street, where he spent a combined six years in corporate finance at Lehman Brothers and Salomon Brothers. "I had a great time on Wall Street, but it didn't satisfy my soul," he says. "I learned from my parents that there are a lot of important things in life you don't measure in dollars and cents."

In 1985 he was tapped to run Yale's failing endowment. It was an unlikely move—Swensen was only thirty-one years old and had never managed an institutional investment portfolio. William Brainerd, who recruited him, admitted, "It looked like an odd choice."

The endowment he inherited was a disaster. From 1968 to 1979, it had lost 45 percent. And the management company specially formed to run it had been fired.

From his university days studying under economist and future Nobel Prize-winner James Tobin, Swensen had become enamored with the idea of diversification. Most institutional portfolios—like the one he had inherited—were almost entirely in stocks and bonds. He argued that such a strategy provided insufficient diversification. Too often, stocks all moved together, and sometimes even together with bonds.

He pioneered an utterly radical idea, eventually dubbed "the Yale Model." It completely revolutionized institutional investing and today is mimicked in some fashion by nearly all institutions.

Swensen realized that investors should de-emphasize stocks and bonds. Investors should instead take advantage of their longtime horizons to invest in hedge funds, real estate, timber, oil and gas, and other alternative investments. His belief was that only by investing in alternatives can you achieve true diversification.

"For a given level of return, if you diversify, you can get that return at lower risk," he said. "For a given level of risk, if you diversify, you can get a higher return. That's pretty cool! Free lunch!"

On a related but equally revolutionary note, he saw the lack of liquidity common in alternative assets to be a benefit, not a liability, because liquidity was mostly unneeded and came at the cost of higher returns.

Swensen's endowment began outperforming every peer and every benchmark. He grew the portfolio from $1.3 billion to $31 billion—making Yale one of the wealthiest schools in the US. The endowment's annual income grew from $45 million per year to $1.6 billion per year. Over his thirty-five-year tenure, Swensen's annual returns were 13.1 percent, during a period in which a standard 60/40 stocks/bonds portfolio earned 8.8 percent.

To put that in context, it's like starting with a $100,000 portfolio that is producing $3,400 per year and growing that to $2.4 million, *while* producing $123,000 per year in income.

What makes Swensen's record astonishing is that while Yale's returns were higher than a normal stocks/bonds portfolio, they were generated with *less risk* and *lower volatility*.

WHY THIS BOOK MATTERS

This book will change your life by changing your financial future.

As we noted above, David Swensen pioneered the Yale Model that is mimicked today by all the world's ultrawealthy. It was revolutionary. And now we will show you exactly how he was able to earn 13.1 percent returns at a time when others made 8.8 percent—with less risk and lower volatility. We will show you how to access the same investments and utilize the same strategies that he and the ultrawealthy use. We will show you the mathematics behind why it works. And we will show you how to implement the same structuring and tax-saving strategies they do.

Higher returns matter. Compounding $100,000 for 30 years at 8.8 percent would net you $1.25 million. Not bad. But the same investment, compounding at 13.1 percent, yields $4 million. That difference alone will change your life.

Risk matters. History shows that losses are harder to overcome. In the investing race between the tortoise and the hare, the tortoise definitely wins.

Volatility matters. Have you ever woken up in the morning to 80 percent losses in a large stock holding? I have. Not only is it emotionally wracking, but it is also very difficult to recover from financially. We will show you the surprising math behind volatility.

Taxes matter. That $100,000 investment earning 13.1 percent per year? If you pay 40 percent taxes every year on your gains, your $4 million gain drops to just $967,000.

Contrary to what you might believe, these investments and strategies are real and are accessible to regular folks. At first glance some things might seem complicated, but we will show you how to navigate them and succeed as a billionaire-like investor.

THE MIRACLE OF COMPOUNDING

Albert Einstein is often attributed with saying, "The most powerful force in the universe is compound interest." He is also said to have referred to it as one of the greatest "miracles" known to man, with the popular quote, "Compound interest is the eighth wonder of the world. He who understands it, earns it ... he who doesn't ... pays it."

Regardless of its origin, the principle behind these words holds undeniable truth. Let's look at a couple of quick examples that illustrate what one of history's greatest minds may have been alluding to.

Let's say you had a magic penny that doubled in value every day. On day two, it would be worth $0.02, day three $0.04, and so on. On day thirty, it would be worth $5.4 million. And on day sixty, $5.7 quadrillion.

Let's go the other way. Say, you were Jesus Christ, and two thousand years ago you started with a penny and put it in a bank where you earned a mere 5 percent return. In the year 2000, your penny would be worth $473 sextillion. That's $473 billion trillion.

These two extreme examples point out the dual factors that drive compound interest. The first is the *rate of return*. Obviously, the higher the rate, the more rapidly compounding happens. The second is *time*. And it really doesn't matter how modest the interest rate is—if there is enough time, the results become astronomical.

> **INVESTING KEY #1**
> Compounding is the key to building wealth.

Compounding is the key the ultrawealthy use to build wealth—and you can make it work for you too.

But there is a catch.

Volatility Destroys Compounding

Let's consider two examples. In the first scenario, you start with $100,000 and compound that every year at 9 percent. In the second scenario, you start with the same $100,000, and your returns fluctuate up and down but *average* 10 percent. Which is better?

Here's the first example:

Year	Rate	Amount	Year	Rate	Amount
		100,000			
1	9%	109,000	16	9%	397,031
2	9%	118,810	17	9%	432,763
3	9%	129,503	18	9%	471,712
4	9%	141,158	19	9%	514,166
5	9%	153,862	20	9%	560,441
6	9%	167,710	21	9%	610,881
7	9%	182,804	22	9%	665,860
8	9%	199,256	23	9%	725,787
9	9%	217,189	24	9%	791,108
10	9%	236,736	25	9%	862,308
11	9%	258,043	26	9%	939,916
12	9%	281,266	27	9%	1,024,508
13	9%	306,580	28	9%	1,116,714
14	9%	334,173	29	9%	1,217,218
15	9%	364,248	30	9%	1,326,768

After 30 years of steady, boring compounding at 9 percent, you have about $1.3 million. Not bad.

But you're not satisfied with a boring 9 percent. You want to swing for the fences. You make 50 percent in the first year! But the next year, you lose 30 percent. It's okay, your average return is 10 percent. You repeat this pattern for the next twenty-eight years. You have done much better than the boring investor because you averaged a 10 percent return. And you had incredible 50 percent returns in half of those years! Let's look:

Year	Rate	Amount	Year	Rate	Amount
		100,000			
1	50%	150,000	16	-30%	147,746
2	-30%	105,000	17	50%	221,618
3	50%	157,500	18	-30%	155,133
4	-30%	110,250	19	50%	232,699
5	50%	165,375	20	-30%	162,889
6	-30%	115,763	21	50%	244,334
7	50%	173,644	22	-30%	171,034
8	-30%	121,551	23	50%	256,551
9	50%	182,326	24	-30%	179,586
10	-30%	127,628	25	50%	269,378
11	50%	191,442	26	-30%	188,565
12	-30%	134,010	27	50%	282,847
13	50%	201,014	28	-30%	197,993
14	-30%	140,710	29	50%	296,990
15	50%	211,065	30	-30%	207,893

With all your hard work, you managed to end up with just $208,000—not even one-sixth of Mr. Boring.

What happened?

> **INVESTING KEY #2**
> Volatility destroys compounding.

It's the math. Let's say you start with $100,000, then lose 50 percent, leaving you $50,000. If the next year you gain 50 percent, you will have $75,000—not $100,000. After losing 50 percent, you must earn 100 percent to break even.

Losses are far, far more impactful than gains. This is why the old adage says, "The first rule of making money is not losing money." Mathematically, minimizing losses is far more important than maximizing gains. It is important that you understand this axiom—and that it's not a platitude or an opinion. It's mathematics. This is the first and most important key on your journey to wealth creation—to stop making risky bets.

This is why volatility is so important. The next time someone mentions Einstein's quote about compounding interest, answer them by saying, "Unless there's volatility!"

Let's look at the volatility of some of the largest, safest, income-oriented stocks and bonds in figure 1. The gray on the top is the dividend yield. The light gray is the average volatility between the years 2000–2023. And the dark gray is the largest drawdown in that period. Look at EQR, a real estate investment trust that owns apartments. You might think it would be very safe, and yet while earning 4.6 percent in dividends, it subjects its investors to an average volatility of almost 23 percent annually and a max drawdown of nearly 70 percent. Anyone who has been in the stock market for any period of time has felt the sting of these sudden and often irrational losses.

> **INVESTING KEY #3**
> Minimizing losses is far more important than maximizing gains.

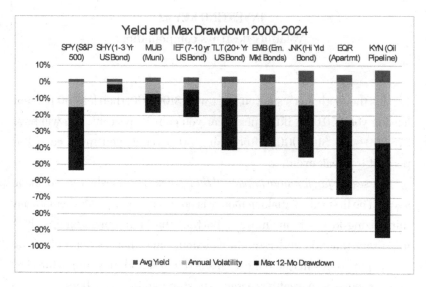

Figure 1: Income Stock Yields and Drawdowns

THE POWER OF PRIVATE ALTERNATIVES

This book is about the power of private alternatives. David Swensen's performance was not an anomaly; it was not luck—it was mathematics. It's what happens when you harness the full power of compounding by achieving true diversification with private alternatives.

Data from iCapital confirms Swensen's results. Figure 2 shows the relative outperformance of alts compared with 60/40 portfolios (60 percent stocks, 40 percent bonds) between 2007 and 2023. And figure 3 shows that alts have suffered far less in drawdowns when compared to stocks and bonds.

THE BILLIONAIRE INVESTOR 27

An allocation to alts would have improved outcomes for a 60/40 Portfolio since 2007
Growth of $1 million from different portfolio allocations, Q3 2007 – Q3 2023

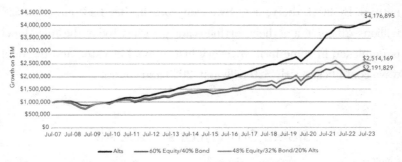

Figure 2: An Allocation to Alts Improves Outcomes for 60/40 Portfolios

Alts have performed well when 60/40 portfolios have fallen
Maximum drawdown of a diversified alts portfolio during 60/40 drawdowns, Q3 2007 – Q3 2023

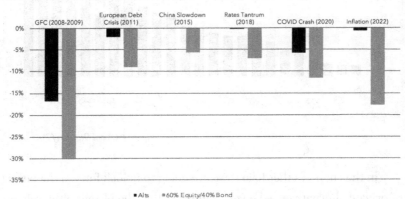

Figure 3: Alts Have Performed Well When 60/40 Portfolios Have Fallen

Swensen's success was a bombshell in the world of the ultrawealthy. In 2001, public pension funds had just 9 percent of their assets in alternatives. By 2021, the year of Swensen's death, they had plowed in $18 trillion—29 percent of their portfolios and growing. Today, the Yale Model is mimicked in some form by every institutional investor, and the tidal wave continues: nearly $20 trillion in 2023 and counting.

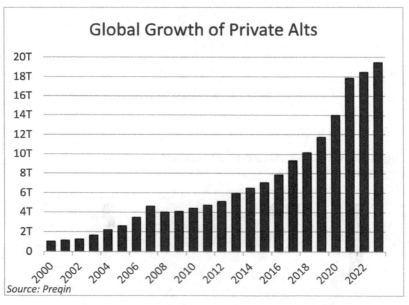

Figure 4: Global Growth of Private Alts

In the chapters that follow, we are going to unlock for you the power of private alternatives—the very same alts that the ultrawealthy rely on to generate higher returns with less risk and less volatility.

So, we know that billionaires think a lot about diversification and reducing risk. But you might be surprised to learn a few other ways billionaires think differently from the rest of us.

CHAPTER 2

WHAT MAKES BILLIONAIRES DIFFERENT FROM YOU AND ME

"It's not how much money you make, but how much money you keep, how hard it works for you, and how many generations you keep it for."
- Robert Kiyosaki

Billionaires act very differently from you and me in their financial lives, and it's not just because they're rich. It's because they know something that many of us don't. And contrary to what you might believe, you too can master the same strategies.

BILLIONAIRES INVEST 50–60 PERCENT IN PRIVATE ALTERNATIVES

From the previous chapter, we've learned that alternatives can give you higher returns with lower risk and less volatility. So, it's not surprising that billionaires love alternatives. In fact, billionaires *allocate 50–60 percent of their investments to alternative investments.*

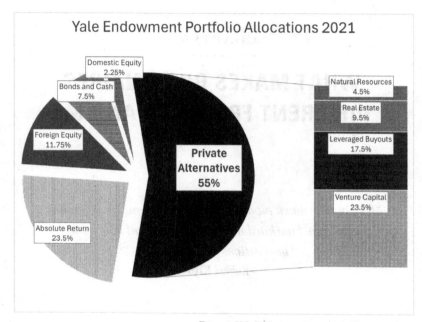

Figure 5: Yale Endowment Investment Allocations, 2021

This pie chart shows the Yale Endowment's recent allocations: 79 percent into alternative investments.

What about the larger universe of wealthy investors? Most of the ultrawealthy invest through "family offices." According to UBS's Global Family Offices survey, the world's wealthy are allocating the same way—59 percent into private alternatives.

Want more proof? Tiger 21 is a group of 1,300 family offices and wealthy individuals with at least $20 million in investable assets. They regularly publish their investors' allocations. You can see the recent data below. They too allocate heavily to alternatives—58 percent.

In contrast, small individual investors are under-allocated to this game-changing strategy. According to McKinsey, *individual investors hold an average of just 2 percent of their wealth in alternatives.*[1]

Two percent!

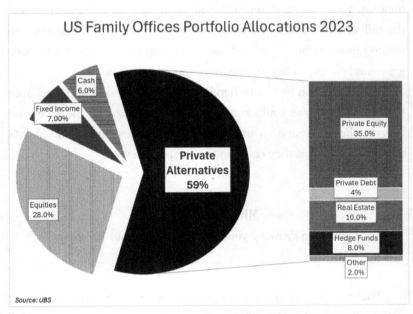

Figure 6: US Family Offices Portfolio Allocations 2023

But that's rapidly changing. In 2012 and again in 2020, the SEC changed the rules to allow greater access to private alts.

Why don't individual investors pursue private alts? Most believe they are out of reach—though they are not. It is mostly due to a knowledge gap, and that's what we aim to help overcome—keep reading! Individual investors can follow the billionaires' methodologies and capture the same extraordinary benefits. By the end of this book, you will have the know-how to successfully follow their example and achieve the same extraordinary results.

BILLIONAIRES FOCUS ON GROWING THEIR BALANCE SHEET, NOT THEIR INCOME STATEMENT

One major difference between the billionaire investor and the typical investor is a key mindset. Smaller investors have an *income statement* mindset. Your income statement shows your *income*, your *expenses*, and the difference between the two: your *net income*. They focus both on making more money—working harder, getting promotions, taking side gigs—and saving money, to maximize their net income.

Billionaires, on the other hand, have a *balance sheet* mindset. Your balance sheet shows your *assets* and your *liabilities*, and the difference between the two: your *net worth*. They focus on buying and building assets and businesses that they can grow and maximize value.

> **MINDSET SHIFT #1**
> Focus on growing your net worth, not your income.

This mindset, by the way, is the reason billionaires pay less taxes, because balance sheet growth is not taxed, while income growth is. We'll share more about this and other billionaire tax strategies in chapter 13.

Smaller investors can move from an income statement mindset to a balance sheet mindset by *using their income to buy and build assets that increase in value*. By doing this year after year, over time your assets will grow, and eventually your investment income will exceed your earned income.

BILLIONAIRES LOVE DEBT

Many of my friends are working hard to get out of debt. They're trying to pay off their mortgages and credit cards and become 100 percent debt free. Popular teachers like Dave Ramsey teach that debt is slavery and should be avoided at all costs.

It may surprise you to learn that billionaires have no such qualms. In fact, most of them love debt and use it to their advantage.

First, they use it to pay less taxes. We'll show you this, too, in chapter 13.

Second, they use it to leverage their investments. Adding a bit of leverage to an investment can greatly enhance returns while increasing risk only slightly. It's smart. Obviously too much leverage can make an investment very risky, so we want to avoid that. I have often said debt is like a fire. Fire can burn your house down, but it can also cook a great steak. Debt should be respected but never feared. Fearing debt is buying a ticket on the poverty train.

Debt is not evil—far from it. If I lend you a dollar, to you that dollar is a debt, but to me that same dollar is an asset. Even if you deposit a dollar in your bank, it goes on the bank's balance sheet as a debt. All debt is someone else's asset. If you argue against debt, then by definition you are arguing against savings.

Debt allows capital to flow from where it is underutilized to where it can be utilized. As such, debt is the lifeblood of the financial system and is responsible for the incredible wealth produced by capitalism over the centuries.

Here are the three principles of smart investment debt. First, make sure that no matter what, you will be able to ***service the debt***. That means the income from the investment, or from other sources, will always be enough to make the debt payments. As long as the payments are made, you are not in danger of losing the investment to your lenders. The second principle is ***not borrowing too much***. For example, if you think your investment could drop 35 percent in value in the most extreme case, then don't borrow more than 65 percent on that investment. That way you'll never be underwater to your lenders and some equity will remain even in such an extreme scenario. Third, do the math on ***variable interest rates***. During the Great Interest Rate Hike of 2023, the Fed raised rates eleven times—hurting many investors who had foolishly assumed rates would stay low forever.

So, investment debt, if used at moderate levels, is simply smart. But what about consumer debt, like credit cards? The conventional wisdom from financial gurus tells us to avoid credit cards like the plague—but that's not always true.

What matters is *what you use credit cards for*. If you use credit cards to buy things you can't afford, then you are certainly asking for trouble.

But in my earlier years, my income fluctuated wildly (the life of a serial entrepreneur!), and I used credit cards to even out the lean months from the plentiful. Credit cards allowed me to raise my family without stress, and to this day, I am grateful that I could borrow money based on my signature alone.

Credit cards can also be a legitimate way to build a business. When one of my friends, who was a missionary, exited the mission field, he returned to the US with nothing. He used some eighty credit cards to begin fixing and flipping houses. Today he has a multimillion-dollar real estate portfolio that's doing extremely well—and zero credit card debt. Obviously, this is not for everyone, but being able to borrow money on just a signature and a promise to repay is an incredible privilege, and an incredible opportunity if you can manage it wisely.

Debt is a tool of the wealthy. They use it wisely to build wealth, and you can too.

BILLIONAIRES LOVE INFLATION

While the little guy suffers from inflation, billionaires profit from it. Let me show you how.

At 8 percent annual inflation, in ten years the value of an asset will roughly double, and the value of money will drop by half. So, a smart strategy is to buy assets that will increase in value from inflation, using debt, which will decrease in value from inflation. For example, if you buy an apartment complex for $10 million, at 8 percent inflation, you could expect your rental income to double in ten years and thus double the value of the property as well. Your $10 million investment would be worth $20 million. And on the other side, if you borrowed $7 million to buy that property, the value of that debt drops in half during the same time. If you sold it, you would turn your $3 million equity investment into $13 million in ten years—a 433 percent return—*from inflation alone*. The numbers work at any level of inflation. At 4 percent inflation, double the time frame to twenty years, etc.

Here's an even crazier (but true!) illustration. Around 2006, a friend of mine from Zimbabwe foresaw inflation on the horizon and borrowed $300,000 from a local bank to buy a 6,000-square-foot Mediterranean-style mansion. The next year, Zimbabwe experienced historic hyperinflation. I visited during this time, and I remember filling grocery bags with cash just to buy a tank of gas! Two years later, he paid off his mortgage with a handful of worthless cash, and today owns that mansion debt free.

Inflation is a massive transfer of wealth from savers to borrowers. Thus, in inflationary times you want to be a borrower (and another reason why you shouldn't be afraid of debt).

INVESTING KEY #4
Inflation is another way to tap the miracle of compounding.

It's beyond the scope of this book to explain why, but you should be aware that in a fractional reserve banking system, as exists today in every country in the world with a central bank, some inflation will be a constant fixture in the economy. Thus, you should always be positioned to profit from it by owning assets that will benefit from inflation and borrowing modestly against them.

If inflation is low, you might think it's not important to consider. But it still makes sense to position your portfolio to capture it. Back to that

$10 million apartment complex: If inflation increases by just 2 percent per year, in ten years the value of that investment will go up by 22 percent, even if nothing else happens. At 3 percent inflation, you would gain 34 percent; and at 4 percent inflation, you would be up 48 percent. Not bad.

As you can see from this little example, *inflation is actually another way to tap the miracle of compounding*—and even low levels of inflation compound over time.

BILLIONAIRES PAY LITTLE IN TAXES

The tax systems of the United States and virtually every other country favor certain categories of income over others. Favored income categories include business income and investment income. It is a simple matter to structure your investments in such a way as to minimize your taxes. We will show you how in chapter 13.

MINDSET SHIFT #2

Most work for their money, but billionaires make their money work for them.

BILLIONAIRES MAKE THEIR MONEY WORK FOR THEM

Most people spend their life working for their money. But billionaires make their money work for them. Obviously, this is easier with larger numbers, but it's a principle everyone should follow: *Put your money to work*.

I love what famous *Shark Tank* investor Kevin O'Leary says: "Here's how I think of my money—as soldiers—I send them out to war every day. I want them to take prisoners and come home, so there's more of them."[2]

It is a mindset shift—our second major mindset shift. Before we move on from this chapter, take a moment and decide that you will learn how to make your money work for you. Even if it's just small amounts at the beginning, this mindset will change the way you invest and will help you become a better investor and multiply wealth.

INVESTING IN INVESTING

Doctors and lawyers spend eight years learning their craft—that's roughly sixteen thousand hours. But few spend more than a few minutes to understand what to *do* with their money—even though *your money has far greater earning power than you do.*

> **MINDSET SHIFT #3**
> **Learning to invest is your most important investment in time.**

Let's say our doctor was able to earn $400,000 per year over her forty-year career. She would earn $16 million total—a good investment in time and money.

Let's say she saved 20 percent—$80,000 per year—and earned a 5 percent return on that. After forty years, she would be worth $9 million. But let's say she invested one hour each week to learn about investing—2,000 hours over forty years, an eighth of the time she spent to become a doctor—and as a result was able to earn a 10 percent return on her investments. Her savings would then turn into $35 million—almost four times the return on the lower investment above and *double her earnings from her medical career.*

And if she read this book, regularly listened to the *Invest Like a Billionaire* podcast, attended investing conferences, and networked with other investors, and was able to earn 15 percent returns, she would be worth $142 million—fifteen times higher than the first return above and *eight times what she earned as a doctor.*

Annual Savings	Annual Return	Net Worth After 40 Years
$80,000	5%	$9,663,982
$80,000	10%	$35,407,404
$80,000	15%	$142,327,225

Spending one-eighth of the time spent on your career to earn eight times more—again shows why perhaps this book might be one of the most important you will ever read.

Building wealth is one thing, but who should you trust to help you do so? Before you entrust your money to a professional, you should know how the game is played.

CHAPTER 3
---

7 THINGS YOUR FINANCIAL ADVISOR WILL NEVER TELL YOU

*"The most contrarian thing of all is not
to oppose the crowd but to think for yourself."*
- Peter Thiel

A question probably burning in your mind right now is, *Why haven't I been told about private alternatives?* The answer is not what you might think—that they are simply not available to smaller investors. They are.

To answer this question, we will need to look at the financial advisory system. Financial advisors are important and helpful and, by and large, good people. I have a financial advisor. But the financial advisory system is also flawed, and in a most important way: *They will generally not help you with private alternatives.*

Here is what happened to me.

When we started our firm Aspen Funds, we were passionate about the power of private alternatives and looked for as many avenues as possible to tell folks about them. I have an indelible memory of one of our earliest strategies. We found a firm that mailed flyers to wealthy individuals and guaranteed to fill fifty seats in a top steakhouse with qualified investors for an evening of (free) fine food and a pitch of our alternative investments.

Everything went precisely as planned. The room was filled; they were indeed all qualified; and they listened intently. We plied them with our charts and graphs, our team, our track record, and our offerings. Afterward, people were universally wowed. The first sentences out of their mouths were things like, "This is amazing!" "I have never heard about such investments," "This is just what I need," and "I'm definitely interested."

The second thing out of their mouths was one of two comments: "I need to show this to my financial advisor," or "I need to find a financial advisor, so I can show this to them." We paid for two such events, a hundred people in total. We were optimistic that we could help them by placing their capital into great products and helping our business grow too. How many investors did we get?

Zero.

What happened? To understand, we need to look at some of the surprising ways the financial advisory system works

#1 FEW ADVISORS KNOW PRIVATE ALTS

The number one answer may surprise you: *Most investment advisors know very little about alternatives*. The advisory system is designed entirely around traditional financial products—stocks, bonds, and insurance.

Advisory firms come in two main flavors: registered investment advisors (RIAs) and broker-dealers (BDs). The rather surprising thing about them is that *neither requires knowledge of alternatives*. There is a license available that focuses on alts (the Series 82), but it is very rare to find an advisor with this qualification. Years ago, I decided to study to become an RIA. I was shocked to discover the discussion of alternatives was covered in just a few pages—not enough to convey even a basic understanding of them.

Before we move on, here's a quick overview of the two types of advisory firms and their differences:

Registered Investment Advisors (RIAs—Series 65). RIAs can be independent, that is, not working under a large financial firm. Legally, they are your *fiduciaries*, which means they are required to advise you in your best interest, and strict care must be taken to avoid conflicts of interest.

RIAs are fee-based—they typically charge fees based on a percentage of "assets under management" or AUM, often in the 1–2 percent range. A few charge hourly or fixed monthly fees. The latter arrangements are favored by the ultrawealthy because they are cheaper. Some may also charge flat fees for financial planning services.

Broker-dealers (BDs—Series 7). These are typically the larger investment firms. They are not fiduciaries, operating under the looser standard of *suitability*. This means their advice must meet your needs, but they may direct you to products that earn higher fees or commissions, and they are not required to disclose conflicts of interest or make you aware of cheaper or better alternatives.

#2 ADVISORS DIRECT YOU TO IN-HOUSE PRODUCTS

All the large broker-dealer firms have in-house products that might include mutual funds, annuities, insurance products, bonds, commodities pools, and even ETFs. These are typically higher-fee products that include sales commissions or management fees to the firm.

Advisors for these firms have sales quotas requiring them to sell certain amounts of in-house products to stay employed.

#3 ADVISORS ARE PLATFORM RESTRICTED

Advisors operate on an investment platform. They select the investment products from this platform and place the trades into this platform. The platform generates investment reports and calculates and deducts advisor fees and commissions.

Many advisors are not permitted to invest your funds outside the platform. Others are allowed, but it is very difficult. Restrictions vary widely by firm. Some RIAs have little to no restrictions, while some BDs are 100 percent restricted.

This is important because most private alts are not listed on these platforms. Most private alts accept new investors only for the first two to three months. It takes too long and is too difficult for sponsors to make their products available on all the various platforms, so they don't bother.

Investing off-platform means the advisor cannot charge their fees, does not earn commissions, cannot control or trade those investments, cannot monitor their performance, and cannot give you reports. It's simply easier for them to keep everything on their platform.

Also, investing in a private alt requires you to sign subscription documents, withdraw cash, and wire it away from accounts the advisor controls. It is inconvenient, and most advisors are understandably reluctant and will try to dissuade you from doing so. After all, if it's going outside them, why do you need them?

In addition, private alts are a bit of a "black box." It is difficult for advisors to get comfortable with them, especially when compared to a stock like IBM, Apple, or an index fund. If those drop in value, the advisor can't be blamed. But if they recommend a private alt, and it loses money, your advisor has some liability and egg on their face. This doesn't necessarily mean the alt is riskier, but that more blame can be assigned. This is another reason why few advisors will recommend alts.

#4 FIDUCIARIES CAN EARN COMMISSIONS

It may seem a little counterintuitive—how can a fiduciary, who is required to act in your best interest, receive commissions on what they sell you? Is it in your best interest to pay commissions?

Commissions can vary widely: from zero for purchasing stocks or ETFs, for example, to 1-10 percent for annuities, to as much as 300 percent of first-year premiums for certain insurance products.

Advisors are obviously incentivized to sell you a high-commission product versus a low-commission product. However, as a fiduciary they are not permitted to let commissions influence their advice. It is clearly a conflict of interest, but a perfectly legal one.

RIAs are required to disclose the types of commissions they receive. You can read this in the Form ADV that they file with regulators which they are required to make public (look for your firm's ADV at https://adviserinfo.sec.gov). However, when making a specific proposal, they are not required to disclose to you the specific commissions they will receive or how much those commissions are.

#5 ADVISORS CAN MARK UP PRODUCTS

Another way advisory firms can get paid is by marking up products. This is most common in bonds. Your advisor may sell you a bond's "coupon," the yield paid on the bond, but mark up the price you pay for the bond. Again, a conflict of interest, but perfectly legal.

#6 PRIVATE ALTS OFFERED BY ADVISORS ARE FAT WITH FEES

Most advisors know they are behind the curve on private alts, and some, especially larger brokerage firms and private banks, offer alternatives. But the offerings are often sponsored by affiliate entities, are laden with fees, and are rarely the best opportunities in the category. They are trying to satisfy the investor's interest without actually giving them complete or great options. Frankly, the worst private alts I have seen have all come from advisors.

#7 ADVISORS CANNOT SHARE PROFITS

In the world of private alts, it is common for the manager to share in the success of their investments—it's called "promote" or "carried interest." The idea is that they share in the profits they create. The manager only makes money when you make money, and the more you make, the more they make. To the average person, this seems sensible because it creates an alignment of interests.

It may surprise you to learn that while advisors can earn fees from sales and for managing your account, they cannot earn fees based on *performance*—it's illegal. Whether they invest your money into something that earns 20 percent per year or something that earns 2 percent per year, their compensation must be the same.

To the normal person, this is very counterintuitive. Most businesses pay their employees bonuses, and give raises and promotions based on *performance*. They do this to create alignment of interests. But again, this is illegal for your advisor.

Here's the point: *Your advisor is not incentivized to make you money*. Nor are they incentivized to prevent you from losing your money. They are incentivized to keep you just happy enough to not move your money away. One of my friends is a very successful advisor. His primary strategy was to construct portfolios such that he never received a client phone call. He said investors called mostly when their portfolios went down, and thus his main goal was to build portfolios that never dipped. This is not all bad—we have already learned that losses are more important than gains. But if he told his investors that he didn't really care how much they made, just how much they lost, I'm sure most of them would be appalled and leave him. Clearly, their interests are not aligned.

When I first learned of this rule, I was astonished. Why would they codify such a gross misalignment of interests? But it does make sense. The authorities created this structure because they do not want advisors incentivized to take risks with their clients' money.

Many argue this system is good. I would argue that it has good elements, but it is also flawed. It tends to make advisors more risk-averse than they should be and even *disincentivizes* them from making optimal risk-adjusted returns—the holy grail of smart investors.

TAKING CONTROL OF YOUR MONEY

I shared our story earlier about when we invited one hundred people to a free steak dinner and to learn about private alts. When they sought advice from their financial advisors, not a single one ended up moving forward.

Given what you now know about financial advisors, that probably doesn't surprise you.

MINDSET SHIFT #4
Billionaires don't outsource control of their money.

But really, the most surprising thing was that no one felt qualified to take control of their own finances. They chose to be passive, entrusting others with decisions about their money—others whose interests, as we've seen, aren't aligned with theirs. Is that really a risk you're willing to take with your financial future?

Would you outsource your career choices? Let someone choose your next job for you? Or decide your educational path? How about your relationships—would you outsource your choice of a spouse? Or your friendships? As we have shown, your financial choices are just as important as your career and your relationships. You need to be involved in them.

On the other hand, *billionaires don't outsource control of their money*. They *do* hire professionals to help, but they also take the time to educate themselves—and they remain the "CEO" of their money. You should be the CEO of your finances too. Yes, get help, get advice, but above all, get smart yourself. Don't let "investment professionals" tell you that it's too complicated or difficult for you to understand. You can do it. No one cares about your money as much as you do—*no one*.

A fourth mindset shift is necessary: *Take ownership of your money*. That doesn't mean you have to be an expert in everything, but it means you take the time to research, listen, learn, ask a lot of questions, and maybe even do your own calculations and spreadsheets. Because you are reading this book, you are probably already doing some of this—if so, congratulations!

FORGING YOUR OWN PATH

Clearly, then, the existing financial advisory infrastructure is not set up to help you with private alts. You may be warned off, cajoled, and you will nearly always be steered away from them. That is changing; every year more advisors embrace private alts, but it is still a small minority. Unless you have found one of these "unicorn" advisors who loves private alts, you will have little choice but to forge your own path.

In spite of these headwinds, the use of private alts among individual investors is rapidly growing—over 15 percent per year according to Preqin.[3] These are the souls who are forging their own path. They are putting in the effort to learn and master private alts, just like the ultrawealthy. This is why this book is important. Research shows that two-thirds of people hire financial advisors for emotional reasons.[4] Don't be one of them—don't be afraid to learn and take charge of your finances.

Advisors play an important role and can be incredibly helpful. As I said, I have one. But no one cares about your money as much as you do. Billionaires take lots of advice, but they don't outsource control of their money—and neither should you.

Next, let's examine the stock market—the smaller investor's main investment game, but one which the ultrawealthy approach in a much more targeted way.

CHAPTER 4

WHAT BILLIONAIRES KNOW ABOUT THE STOCK MARKET

"The difference between playing the stock market and the horses is that one of the horses must win."
- **Joey Adams**

We have seen how the ultrawealthy lean heavily toward alternatives to lower their risk and achieve higher returns. They invest 20-30 percent in the public stock market—while smaller investors use the public markets almost exclusively. Billionaires know that the public markets and standard 60/40 portfolios (60 percent stocks, 40 percent bonds) alone will not allow them to build a high-return, low-risk portfolio.

The public markets offer some powerful advantages: liquidity; the ability to move quickly and deploy large amounts of capital; trading with the click of a button; and access to some of the world's largest and best companies. But the public markets also come with some serious limitations and drawbacks that the ultrawealthy are well aware of—which is why they use them in such a limited fashion.

So why do billionaires keep just 20-30 percent of their capital in the public markets? What do they know that the little guy doesn't?

HOW THE PUBLIC MARKETS WORK

First, a little primer on how the public markets work.

"Going public" is when a company lists its shares (or its debt) for sale on a public stock exchange. It is a very arduous and expensive process. Companies do this for one main reason: access to large amounts of cheap capital. At its initial public offering (IPO), a company earmarks some of its shares for sale, typically 15–35 percent. Brokers line up potential buyers, and when there is enough momentum, the shares are listed on the exchange and the purchases are executed. When those initial shares are sold, all of that cash (less commissions) goes into the company's coffers—millions and even billions of dollars of essentially free money—for expansion, R&D, or whatever the company wants.

Thereafter, those original shares continue to articulate among investors. The company can repeat this process, putting more shares into circulation and getting more cash. Shares are also added to the market if the stock splits (for example, one share is exchanged for two shares). Shares are removed from the market in a reverse split, or when the company does a stock buyback (using company cash to buy back their own shares). The number of shares in circulation is referred to as the *float*. The total value of the company is called the *market cap*, which is the share price times the total number of shares.

The exchanges take bids (offers to buy a certain number of shares at a certain price) and asks (offers to sell a certain number of shares at a certain price) and match them, hundreds, or thousands of times per second. If buyers flood in, they overwhelm the available sellers and prices rise, presumably attracting more sellers at the higher price. The reverse happens if sellers flood the market.

The point is this: Every stock is traded in a *continuous, live public auction*, and the stock market is a collection of *thousands of continuous, live public auctions*.

Volatility

One of the most appealing features of the public markets is their liquidity. Being able to sell at a moment's notice is wonderful—but it comes with a serious drawback: volatility. You may indeed be able to sell any time you like, but you may not like the price you get.

Figure 8 shows the danger. In those twenty-four years, the S&P 500 experienced eight drawdowns of 20 percent or more, including four of 35 percent or more and one of almost 55 percent.

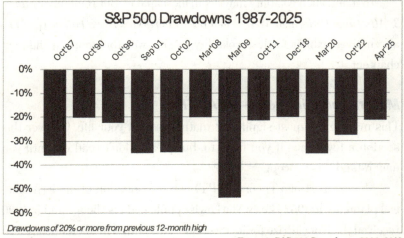

Figure 8: S&P 500 Drawdowns 2000–2023

Volatility Extremes

But what's even more concerning is that market volatility is far more extreme than most experts acknowledge. According to traditional mathematical models, the S&P 500 should never have moved up or down by 5 percent in a single day over the past century—yet it has happened 164 times. And then there's Black Monday, October 19, 1987, when the market plunged 20 percent in a single day—an event that, based on these models, should be so rare it wouldn't have occurred even once since the beginning of the universe 13.7 billion years ago.[5]

Clearly, the models are flawed—as are the financial constructs built upon them. If you want to dive deeper into this phenomenon, check out Appendix B: *Fat Tails* for a more technical breakdown. Otherwise, just know this: Violent market swings happen far more often than they should, and the wealthiest investors understand this all too well. That's why most billionaires don't entrust the majority of their wealth to the stock market—and neither should you.

To many, such volatility may seem inescapable. But remember *Figure 3: Alts Have Performed Well When 60/40 Portfolios Have Fallen* (p. 27)—alternatives exhibit far less volatility. We'll cover this more in the next chapter.

Modern Portfolio Theory—READ THIS!

This may be the most significant math lesson of your life. Go over this section a few times if you need to, but please don't read on until you understand this concept.

Modern Portfolio Theory (MPT) is the foundation of modern financial planning. In 1952 Harry Markowitz published his theory and in 1990 received the Nobel Prize for its invention. He showed mathematically that *by diversifying into uncorrelated assets, the overall risk was lower than simply a weighted sum of the risks.*

Your brain probably just melted. Let me explain by example. Let's say you hold stocks A, B, C, and D, and each has an annual volatility of 20 percent (that means 70 percent of the time, you expect each of them to gain or lose 20 percent in a year). You might expect your overall portfolio to have 20 percent volatility as well. If A, B, C, and D are correlated, that is what you get.

However, if A, B, C, and D are *uncorrelated* (we'll discuss this in more detail later), *your portfolio volatility will be lower than the average volatility.*

In fact, if they are perfectly uncorrelated, your overall portfolio volatility—I will spare you the math—is half as much, just 10 percent. If you have 16 uncorrelated stocks each with 20 percent volatility, your portfolio volatility drops to 5 percent.

Hello, compounding!

This was the essence of the "free lunch" referred to by Swensen. It was truly groundbreaking. It cannot be overstated how important this is. This is why alternatives should be a cornerstone of your portfolio, because as you will see, they are the most uncorrelated to other asset classes.

> **INVESTING KEY #2**
> If investments are uncorrelated, your portfolio volatility will be lower than average volatility.

There are two mechanisms you can use to tap the power of MPT: *lower correlations* and a *higher number of assets*. The table below illustrates how much reduction in portfolio volatility you can generate with these two levers.

Portfolio Risk Reduction by Increasing Assets and Reducing Correlation

Correlation Between Asset Pairs	Number of Assets in Portfolio				
	2	4	7	10	17
1.0	0%	0%	0%	0%	0%
0.8	-5%	-8%	-9%	-9%	-10%
0.6	-11%	-16%	-19%	-20%	-21%
0.4	-16%	-26%	-30%	-32%	-34%
0.2	-23%	-37%	-44%	-47%	-50%
0.0	-29%	-50%	-62%	-68%	-74%

Figure 9: Reduction in Portfolio Risk by Reducing Correlations and Increasing Number of Assets

Volatility matters a lot. Remember, low volatility is the key that unlocks the magic of compounding. And, as I will show you in a moment, private alts are really the only way to achieve it.

THE DIVERSIFICATION MYTH

Bear with me for one final bit of "mathiness"—there is one more very important concept to understand: the challenge of diversification.[6] If you buy twenty different stocks, you are diversified *only to the degree those stocks move independently from one another*. This concept is called correlation. If two stocks move in perfect unison, they have a correlation of 1.0. If two stocks move together 50 percent of the time, they would have a correlation of 0.5. If two stocks move exactly opposite each other, they would have a correlation of -1.0.

Look at the table in figure 11. It shows the correlations between various asset classes prior to July 2007. The shaded cells show the problem: *Even widely differing asset classes are highly correlated*. Growth, value, small cap, and large cap stocks are more than 75 percent correlated, and nothing is strongly negatively correlated.

But since the Great Financial Crisis in 2007, things have gotten even worse—notice the dramatic increase in correlations. Almost everything is correlated to everything: REITs, high-yield bonds, and commodities used to offer investors some diversification, but no longer (figure 12*)*. And negative correlations have all but disappeared.

In a post-GFC analysis, J.P. Morgan made a few very astute observations regarding market correlations.[7]

1. Correlations have been steadily increasing since 2000.
2. In times of high volatility, correlations increase.
3. In times of high macro uncertainty, correlations increase, because stocks are increasingly driven by macro factors, which are common to all.

Pre-GFC Correlations Between Asset Classes (Jan 1988 - Jul 2007)

	Large Cap	Small Cap	Value	Growth	Developed World	Emerging Markets	Investment Grade Bonds	High Yield Bonds	REITs	Commodities
Large Cap		0.73	0.91	0.94	0.62	0.58	0.18	0.50	0.37	-0.09
Small Cap	0.73		0.71	0.79	0.53	0.62	0.03	0.57	0.53	0.00
Value	0.91	0.71		0.76	0.57	0.56	0.18	0.51	0.51	-0.09
Growth	0.94	0.79	0.76		0.58	0.58	0.13	0.47	0.29	-0.07
Developed World	0.62	0.53	0.57	0.58		0.58	0.06	0.35	0.25	0.01
Emerging Markets	0.58	0.62	0.56	0.58	0.58		-0.05	0.43	0.30	0.04
Investment Grade Bonds	0.18	0.03	0.18	0.13	0.06	-0.05		0.24	0.18	-0.02
High Yield Bonds	0.50	0.57	0.51	0.47	0.35	0.43	0.24		0.44	-0.11
REITs	0.37	0.53	0.51	0.29	0.25	0.30	0.18	0.44		-0.10
Commodities	-0.09	0.00	-0.09	-0.07	0.01	0.04	-0.02	-0.11	-0.10	

Figure 11: Correlations Between Traditional Asset Classes Pre-GFC

Post-GFC Correlations Between Asset Classes (Aug 2007 - Dec 2022)

	Large Cap	Small Cap	Value	Growth	Developed World	Emerging Markets	Investment Grade Bonds	High Yield Bonds	REITs	Commodities
Large Cap		0.91	0.97	0.97	0.88	0.75	0.18	0.74	0.78	0.51
Small Cap	0.91		0.93	0.89	0.80	0.70	0.08	0.73	0.76	0.51
Value	0.97	0.93		0.89	0.87	0.74	0.11	0.74	0.79	0.55
Growth	0.97	0.89	0.89		0.85	0.74	0.23	0.74	0.73	0.48
Developed World	0.88	0.80	0.87	0.85		0.87	0.22	0.78	0.72	0.58
Emerging Markets	0.75	0.70	0.74	0.74	0.87		0.24	0.76	0.63	0.56
Investment Grade Bonds	0.18	0.08	0.11	0.23	0.22	0.24		0.32	0.33	-0.13
High Yield Bonds	0.74	0.73	0.74	0.74	0.78	0.76	0.32		0.74	0.52
REITs	0.78	0.76	0.79	0.73	0.72	0.63	0.33	0.74		0.34
Commodities	0.51	0.51	0.55	0.48	0.58	0.56	-0.13	0.52	0.34	

Figure 12: Correlations Between Traditional Asset Classes Post-GFC

4. Increasing correlations are tied to the increase in ETF and futures volumes. This makes sense since ETFs and futures trade hundreds or even thousands of shares in unison. JPM noted that in 2001, ETFs and futures accounted for around 20

percent of trade volumes, and by 2010, that number had grown to around 60 percent.
5. Immediate access to information and the ability to trade quickly can lead to a "sell everything" herd mentality that can dramatically increase the short-term correlations of assets that aren't normally highly correlated.

With high correlations, you lose the mathematical advantages of portfolio diversification. Your portfolio faces the full brunt of market volatility, and with it, the power of compounding. It is the main reason why the ultrawealthy limit their exposure to the public markets.

THE LIQUIDITY PREMIUM

Another reason the ultrawealthy avoid investing too heavily in public markets—one that was regularly mentioned by David Swensen—is the *liquidity premium*. The concept is this: Because investors prefer liquidity, investments that have greater liquidity trade at a price premium. Conversely, investments without liquidity trade at a discount, resulting in higher returns.

MINDSET SHIFT #5
Calculate your true liquidity needs and place no more than that in more expensive, liquid assets.

According to research by Cambridge Associates, investors have the potential to gain 50–75 basis points (bps) in additional total portfolio returns for every 10 percent of global equity capital that is reallocated to private investments such as private equity and venture capital.[8] Most investors overestimate their need for liquidity. Astute investors make a realistic estimate of their liquidity needs and place no more than that in the more expensive, liquid options. We'll touch more on the advantage of illiquid investments in the next chapter.

BILLIONAIRES DON'T BELIEVE IN EFFICIENT MARKETS

Anyone who has ever attended an in-person, live public auction would have difficulty concluding that it was entirely rational. However, in 1970, Eugene Fama published the Efficient Market Hypothesis (EMH), which did just that. He postulated that information about stocks is continuously digested by the market in real time and acted on by buyers and sellers, and thus stocks *always trade at their fair market value*. EMH remains hotly debated to this day.

EMH concludes that value investing, or any other strategy for that matter, is an exercise in foolishness. According to EMH, it is impossible for anyone to consistently beat the market. However, history has many—like Warren Buffett, John Templeton, Peter Lynch, and Paul Tudor Jones—who year over year beat the market by large margins.

Billionaires have spoken out against EMH. George Soros's principle of fallibility denies EMH when it says, "In situations that have thinking participants, the participants' view of the world is always partial and distorted."[9] Buffett, one of the most successful investors of all time, said, "Observing that the market was *frequently* efficient, EMH adherents went on to conclude incorrectly that it was *always* efficient. The difference between these propositions is night and day."[10] He famously quipped, "I'd be a bum on the street with a tin cup if the markets were always efficient."[11] He said EMH has done a "disservice" to "students and gullible investment professionals who have swallowed" it.[12] Instead, billionaires believe that the markets are partially driven by irrational behavior, incorrect or incomplete information, flawed assumptions, false narratives, and a herd mentality. For them, this creates opportunities.

BUBBLES

According to EMH, irrational "market bubbles" cannot exist. Yet clearly, excessive optimism and pessimism have been at play throughout history, from the tulip mania of 1637 and the South Sea Bubble of 1720 to the dot-com bubble of the late 1990s and the housing bubble of the mid-2000s, to name just a few.

The housing bubble was driven by widespread belief that home prices only went up. It was fueled by lax lending standards and large securitizations of mortgages based on dubious financial models (again, rooted in statistical mathematics that underrepresented fat tail risk). As housing prices soared, more and more people jumped in, convinced they could buy a home, wait a few years, and make substantial profits. The movie version of Michael Lewis's book *The Big Short* includes a memorable scene of a stripper who had become a housing market speculator:

> **Mark Baum:** Okay, look. If home prices don't go up, you are not going to be able to refinance. And you'll be stuck paying whatever your monthly payment is once it jumps up after your teaser rate expires. Your monthlies could go up two-, three-hundred percent.
>
> **Florida Strip Club Dancer:** James says I can always refinance.
>
> **Baum:** Well, he's a liar. Actually, in this particular case, James probably is wrong.
>
> **Dancer:** 200 percent? On all my loans?
>
> **Baum:** What do you mean "all" your loans? We're talking about two loans on one house, right?
>
> **Dancer:** I have five houses ... and a condo.[13]

In every bubble there inevitably emerges a handful of individuals, who, by their genius, or luck, or both, profit immensely from the crash, like Michael Burry in 2008. However, no hedge funds profited from the tech crash of 2001–2002, though Soros claimed to, and in fact most were still overweight in tech.[14] Julian Robertson of Tiger Management tried but went bust betting against tech stocks as the markets ripped higher.[15] I am not aware of any savants with the prescience to profit both from the rise and the demise of any bubble.

Bubbles usually have enough underlying truth and credibility backed by momentum to steamroll skeptics. And bubbles can run higher and longer than imaginable, making shorting them (betting against them) difficult as well. Fed chairman Alan Greenspan called out the "irrational exuberance" of the Internet bubble in 1996, three years before and 340 percent below its eventual peak.[16] For nearly everyone, including the ultrawealthy, bubbles are treacherous and notoriously difficult to spot and profit from. Warren Buffett was famously dumbfounded by the dot-com bubble: While the Nasdaq blazed to new highs, up 145 percent from July 1998 through February 2000, Buffet's Berkshire Hathaway had its worst performance ever, down 45 percent. Even though he was neutral technology stocks, value stocks were getting crushed by sexy tech stocks.

Narrative Driven

In 1997, Amazon went public as "the leading online retailer of books" at $18 per share. At the time, Amazon reported full-year revenue of $15.75 million. Between 1997 and 1999, Amazon's sales rose steadily, but exuberance for its shares rose even faster as the dot-com frenzy mushroomed by December 1999, its shares had split 12-for-1 (three splits) and were up 40x. It wouldn't reach that high again for nearly *ten years*.[17] By October of 2001, less than two years later, the stock had fallen by 95 percent.[18] During that epic price crash, Amazon's revenue continued to rise from $1.64 billion in 1999 to $2.76 billion in 2000 and $3.12 billion in 2001.[19]

What changed in those two years? Did Amazon stumble? Did the promise of the Internet fail? No, the only thing that changed was the *narrative*. The markets turned from excessive optimism to excessive pessimism.

When Amazon reached its 1999 peak, its revenues were $1.64 billion with losses of $719 million. When it finally reached that same valuation again ten years later, its revenues were $34.2 billion—twenty times higher—and it earned $1.15 billion in profits. How could the money-losing 1999 Amazon be valued the same as the profitable and twenty-times-larger 2010 Amazon?

The answer is that the public markets are highly *narrative driven*. When the popular narrative was all about Internet hype, investors stampeded in. When the bubble popped, the popular narrative changed, and investors stampeded out the door as fast as they'd rushed in.

In 2017, Long Island Iced Tea Corp. renamed itself Long Blockchain Corp., causing its stock to surge 200 percent. Every few years, a new narrative gains viral momentum: dot-com, big data, blockchain, IoT, AI—and I'm sure there will be several more in every decade.

Nobel Laureate Robert Shiller argued in his books *Irrational Exuberance* and *Narrative Economics* that humans are story-driven creatures, and compelling narratives can overcome rational analytics. Stories are amplified by news cycles and social media that reinforce popular trends. As the trend develops, more people are drawn into it for fear of missing out (the dreaded FOMO). Eventually narratives tire, are deconstructed, and the trend reverses.

The Harsh Reality of a Bubble

Warren Buffett was not the only guy getting crushed trying to navigate a bubble. In his book *Unconventional Success*, David Swensen analyzed the performance of the top ten tech funds during the dot-com bubble. The first three years, 1997–1999, were stunning, producing an average of 5.8 times the original investment—a compound annual return of 78 percent. The next three years, 2000–2002, were almost a mirror image, producing annual losses of 42 percent. An investor who invested for the full six-year round trip made a little bit of money—a compound annual return of 1.5 percent.

The problem is, *virtually no one did that.*

Swensen's analysis of investment inflows and outflows paints a very sad picture. Most investors started investing too late in the game. And as Internet stocks rose, investors plowed even more cash into them—effectively buying at the top. When the markets turned down, investors held out too long, and in fact even continued to invest more capital, showing the power of narrative even amid face-ripping losses. By the end, on average, *investors had lost 72 percent of their initial investment.*

Adding insult to injury, because the funds churned their portfolio holdings, they generated large capital gains tax liabilities. So even after *losing* 72 percent of their investment, investors paid significant taxes on their *gains*.[20]

EMOTIONAL MISTAKES

The field of behavioral finance studies the role of human emotions in financial behavior. It is utterly fascinating. Institutional investors and professional investors are well aware of these behaviors and often profit from them. However, data shows that smaller, individual investors as a whole succumb to their emotional wiring and are typically very poor investors as a result.

BlackRock[21] and the SEC both published lists of the most common investor pitfalls.[22] I will summarize a few here.

1. **Active Trading.** Data shows that many investors, especially men, trade too actively and speculatively and underperform as a result.
2. **Familiarity Bias.** People prefer to invest in what is familiar, favoring their own country, region, state, or company.
3. **Manias and Panics.** York University economist Brenda Spotton Visano described a financial mania as the "gradual spreading

of speculative euphoria, one that becomes increasingly intense." She explained that mania occurs before, and panic occurs after, "the peak of the business cycle spawned by revolutionary innovation."[23]

4. **Momentum Investing.** Buying securities with high recent returns and selling those with low recent returns.
5. **"Shiny Object" Trading.** Buying and selling without fundamental data, instead following trends, attention-grabbing stocks, stocks in the news, or those that experience abnormal one-day returns or volumes. Studies show that these stocks don't subsequently perform as well as the stocks those same investors sold.[24]
6. **Confirmation Bias.** Investors tend to retain only the information that confirms their investing choices.
7. **Anchoring Bias.** Investors tend to anchor on initial information and interpret any new information in relation to it. One manifestation of this is buying stocks with recent high returns and selling those with low recent returns.
8. **Repetition Bias.** Attributing more credibility to frequently repeated information.
9. **Activity Bias.** The tendency to want to act in difficult times, because activity has a reassuring effect on the mind when we feel under stress.
10. **The Disposition Effect.** The tendency of investors to sell winning positions and to hold on to losing positions. One study showed that in the months following the sale of winning investments, these investments continued to outperform the losing positions still held in the investment portfolio. Loss-averse investors sell high-performing investments hoping to recoup their losses on poor performers but achieving the opposite.[25]

11. **The Herd Effect.** Trusting the judgment of the majority, or those around us, more than our own. Individuals try to conform their opinion to the consensus opinion of the group.
12. **Overconfidence Bias.** My friend Jim Dew, who advises successful entrepreneurs, says this is a big error he often sees—especially when an entrepreneur sells his or her company. Typically, they will invest in a lot of private deals and lose a ton of money because they think they are smarter than they are.
13. **Availability Bias.** When analyzing a private deal, investors focus on the information that is most easily available to them—often from the person trying to raise money for a particular deal.

CONCENTRATION RISK

Another reason sophisticated investors are wary of the stock market is the hidden concentration risk. The most popular investing strategy in recent years is *index investing*—investing in popular indexes, which are groups of stocks. Most indexes have tracking ETFs (exchange-traded funds) that let you buy the entire index in a single stock. The most popular is the S&P 500 Index, and its tracking ETF "SPY," which comprises the largest 500 stocks in the market. These 500 stocks together account for 80 percent of the value of the entire stock market.

What a simple way to get diversification—buy one stock and get exposure to 500 stocks, right?

Not exactly.

The S&P 500 (and most indexes) are *capitalization weighted*—the larger the company, the larger the share of the index they command. The top ten stocks in the S&P 500 represent one-third of the index, and one-fourth of its earnings. That's hardly diversification—you are really just buying a handful of the largest companies.

BEATING THE MARKETS

Earlier I highlighted a few great investors who exploited market inefficiencies to great success. But I also pointed out that they failed to identify or exploit both directions of public market bubbles. They, too, nearly always followed stunning success with equally stunning whiffs in subsequent time periods. If they really were savants, how could this be?

It can be argued that luck was as responsible for their success as skill. In his book *Fooled by Randomness*, Nassim Taleb cleverly pointed out that randomness will masquerade as genius. If you taught 100,000 chimpanzees to type and put them in front of Bloomberg terminals, odds are that one of them would beat the market in an extraordinary way.[26]

The overwhelming evidence (when it comes to public markets) is that very few can beat the averages consistently over time. In Charlie Munger's final interview, he said that times have changed since his early days of picking stocks, and that most people today will be much better off picking an indexed investment rather than trying to beat the market.[27] In the public markets, I challenge the stance that it's a good bet to try to outperform the tax-and-fee drag that active managers face. The public markets have humbled everyone who has attempted to best them.

It's in the world of private investments where performance can be above average. The data proves it—see *Figure 18: Public and Private Manager Dispersion* in the next chapter. If you want to beat the markets and exploit inefficiencies, the private markets are rich hunting grounds.

YOUR PUBLIC MARKETS STRATEGY

How, then, should you approach the public markets? Foremost, abandon the idea of trying to *beat* the averages through active trading. Rather, like the ultrawealthy, *ride* the markets through buy-and-hold strategies.

The public markets constitute an important component of your investment portfolio. But like the ultrawealthy, you should recognize their negatives—volatility, high liquidity premiums, and poor diversification—and utilize them in a limited and targeted fashion.

So, we have seen that the ultrawealthy vastly favor private alts over the public markets, investing twice as much. Now it's time to take a look at *why*.

CHAPTER 5

WHAT MAKES PRIVATE ALTS SO ATTRACTIVE

"The individual investor should act consistently as an investor and not as a speculator."
- Ben Graham

So far, we have looked at what billionaires do and taken a glance at the public markets and their challenges. Now it's time to dive into private alts, why they are so favored by the ultrawealthy, and how they have become one of the fastest-growing segments of finance, attracting nearly $20 trillion.

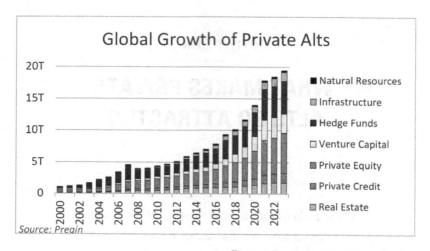

Figure 15: Growth of Private Alts by Asset Class

You've seen how the ultrawealthy allocate their capital. Here is the total size of all private alts globally:

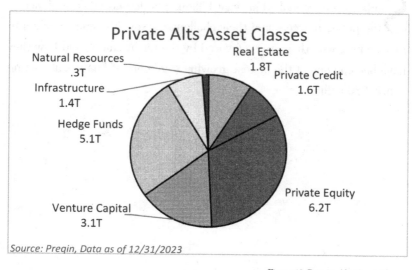

Figure 16: Private Alts Asset Classes

We will dive into each of these asset classes in detail in the next section.

WHAT IS A PRIVATE ALT?

Before we go further, let's look under the hood. What exactly is a private alt?

- A *private alt* is simply a private investment company formed by a sponsor to buy a particular investment asset or group of assets. The sponsor money from investors, invests it, and shares the profits.
- Sometimes the fund doesn't have specific assets to purchase, but a *type* of assets they expect to purchase. This is called a *blind pool*, because you don't know the specific assets that the business will buy.
- *Private* means the investment is not listed on the public markets (you can't buy it on the stock market). Instead, you purchase it by reading and signing the offering documents and then wiring the money to the company. You are then a part owner of the business.
- Most private alts are *closed-end funds*, which accept investment capital for a limited time, invest it, and, after another fixed point in time, liquidate the assets, distribute profits, and shut down the fund. Others are *open-ended funds*, which operate indefinitely, accepting investment capital at regular intervals. These funds typically perform quarterly valuations to adjust the share price and often offer some form of liquidity, allowing you to liquidate your investment on demand.
- The sponsor will regularly send you financial statements and reports updating you on the progress and performance of the business.
- Alts are typically structured as limited liability corporations (LLCs).

- They are typically *manager-managed*, meaning the LLC is managed by the sponsor. The sponsor/manager is called the general partner (GP), and the investors are called limited partners (LPs). Limited partners are so named because they do not share in any liability the business might encounter—things like debts, lawsuits, judgments, or regulatory actions. LPs can lose their investment capital, but no more. GPs, on the other hand, bear full responsibility for things like fraud, negligence, regulatory actions, lawsuits, etc. They often personally guarantee debt.
- LP investors are *passive*—you don't work in or on the business at all; your only contribution is your capital.
- As an LP investor, you are a *business owner*—and as such, at tax time you will receive a Schedule K-1, which is a *partner's share of income, deductions, and credits*. It assigns income and deductions to you according to your percentage ownership in the business. There can be significant benefits to this, as any tax advantages generated by the business are generally passed on directly to you. We'll dive deeper into this in a moment.
- These businesses typically have no employees. The employees of the GP do the necessary work.
- GPs typically charge a variety of fees for their risk and efforts. Fees typically include some kind of fixed fees to help cover overhead, as well as performance-based fees. Fees and profit splits are all clearly delineated in the private placement memorandum (PPM). We'll hit these in detail in chapter 18, "Navigate A PPM In 30 Minutes."
- The *offering documents* are the legal paperwork associated with the investment. They clearly delineate everything discussed above: the asset or assets to be purchased, the strategy and business plan, the plan of distribution, how taxes will work, liquidity options (if any), the reporting and financials that will be sent, the fees and structures, etc.

Private alts, private equity, and *hedge funds* initially may sound mysterious and complicated—but as you can see, they are really not. They are just businesses, like any other, but formed for the purpose of investing money to make profits. And as an investor, you become a part owner of that business.

So why do the ultrawealthy rely so heavily on private alts?

Higher Returns

As we've already touched on, data shows that private alts can generate higher returns than the public markets.

- Recall David Swensen's story in chapter 1: Through private alts, he generated 13.1 percent returns during a time when the standard 60/40 stocks/bonds portfolio earned 8.8 percent.
- *Figure 2: An Allocation to Alts Improves Outcomes for 60/40 Portfolios* (p. 27) shows the significant outperformance of alts since 2007.
- A Cambridge Associates study of institutional investors showed that those with higher allocations to private alts outperformed over five-, ten-, fifteen-, and twenty-year time horizons.[28]
- Data from J.P. Morgan shows that alts produce significantly higher returns and lower volatility.[29] Look at figure 17 below. The open bubbles show 40/60, 60/40, and 80/20 stocks/bonds portfolios in terms of return (vertical axis) and volatility (horizontal axis). The dark bubbles show that adding 30 percent alts to each category moved two of the bubbles up (higher returns) and all three to the left (lower volatility).
- Look at figure 18 below. Private alts can generate significantly higher returns compared to traditional investments.[30] The three bars on the left are public investments—and you can see the range of returns doesn't vary much between managers. The four on the right are alternatives—and the returns range

70 INVEST LIKE A BILLIONAIRE

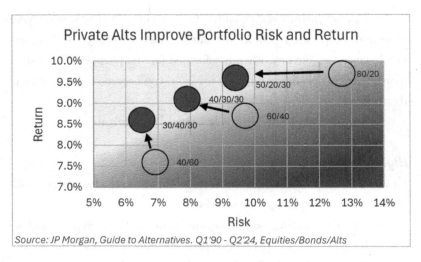

Figure 17: Alternatives and Portfolio Risk / Return

widely based on the manager. In the world of private alts, great managers can generate exceptional returns, and poor managers can generate dismal returns. This chart shows that private sponsors can generate outsized returns—far higher than public investments. With private alts, it is possible to "beat the market" with killer returns.

Private alts can generate higher returns.

- It also illustrates the importance of manager selection when investing in private alts—a topic we will cover in depth in chapter 16, "How to Select an Operator."

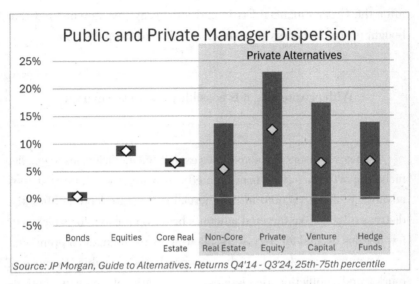

Figure 18: Public and Private Manager Dispersion

How are private alts able to achieve this? Here are several ways.

No Liquidity Premium. In the previous chapter, we discussed the liquidity premium of public investments. Of course, investors prefer liquidity and are willing to pay up for it, which makes public investments more expensive than private investments. An illiquidity discount compensates investors with a higher expected return for investing in less liquid assets. Private alts are inherently less liquid than public investments, so investors expect higher overall returns from private alts.

Opportunistic. Some private alts are *opportunistic*, taking advantage of temporary inefficiencies in markets. For example, after the housing crash of 2008, alts giant Blackstone raised $13 billion from investors to purchase houses at the market bottom, generating impressive returns due to the temporary market dislocation.[31] Our own company, Aspen Funds, has made many opportunistic investments that produced outsized returns, including a distressed debt fund that purchased discounted mortgages after the Great Financial Crisis and an energy investment fund that bought upstream energy production at a time of steep discounts.

> **With private alts, it is possible to "beat the market."**

Niches. Sponsors can sometimes exploit the inefficiencies in smaller niche opportunities. Our firm created a private credit fund that took advantage of the vacuum in commercial real estate lending after the distress of 2023. We targeted amounts below $5 million, for which very few options existed for borrowers, allowing us to command a premium.

Another example of a niche opportunity is cannabis. Because of murky and conflicting regulations, few traditional financing options are available to cannabis companies. Banks won't lend to them. Private lenders and equity providers to cannabis companies have their pick of projects and can command premiums, with the potential for outsized returns for investors.

Tax Efficiency. Private alts are very tax efficient. Most public companies are *double taxed*—the company pays corporate income taxes, then, if they pay dividends to investors, investors are taxed on those dividends (some are not double taxed, like REITs, LLPs/LPs, and UITs). Private alts, however, are *single taxed*. As LLCs, they are *pass-through* entities—they don't pay taxes themselves but pass tax liabilities (and benefits) through to the investors.

Most generate additional tax efficiencies besides single taxation. They can generate long-term capital gains, depreciation, depletion allowances, intangible drilling costs, tax credits, etc. And again, any tax benefits they generate—and most alts do—are passed on directly to the investor.

Better Compounding. As we have shown in chapter 1, the miracle of compounded returns requires low volatility. And private alts have far lower volatility.

Low Volatility

Private alts do not participate in a live, continuous public auction like public equities. This means they generally have little or no liquidity. But it also means they're not subject to the wild swings so common to the stock market. And most, being asset-based, benefit from the generally stable pricing of large assets. Abundant data proves the lower volatility of alts:

- *Figure 25: Private Alts Risk and Return* (p. 90) shows various private alts asset classes and their risk and returns. The upper-left quadrant represents higher returns and lower risk. Every alts class has lower risk than the public markets.
- Recall that *Figure 3: Alts Have Performed Well When 60/40 Portfolios Have Fallen* (p. 27) shows the superior drawdown characteristics of alts.
- *Figure 17: Alternatives and Portfolio Risk / Return* (p. 70) shows the lower volatility of adding alts to a portfolio.
- According to CAIA data: "A 100% alts portfolio, with equal allocations across private equity, private debt, hedge funds, and real assets, incurred maximum drawdowns at least 20% smaller than those of 60/40 portfolio in the trailing 10- and 15-year periods as of the fourth quarter of 2020. The same portfolio had a 10-year and 15-year Sharpe ratio of 1.38 and 0.87, respectively, compared to 0.66 and 0.43 for the 60/40 portfolio."[32] The Sharpe ratio is the standard measure of risk-adjusted returns—and higher is better.

Illiquidity

This may seem counterintuitive: How can the illiquidity of private investments make them attractive?

In the previous chapter, we pointed out that few investors do well in the public markets because their emotional wiring trips them up. This is why low volatility and illiquidity actually result in greater success for individual investors. Low volatility means there are fewer emotional triggers; and illiquidity means you can't act on them even if you wanted to.

Uncorrelated

Recall the most important takeaway of Modern Portfolio Theory (MPT): Overall portfolio volatility can be reduced below the average volatility of the individual investments if the investments are uncorrelated.

Private alts have low and even negative correlations to other investments, including the stock market. *Figure 26: Private Alts S&P 500 Correlation and Sharpe Ratio* (p. 90) shows the correlations of alts to the S&P 500 on the horizontal axis; and the Sharpe Ratio, a popular measure of risk-adjusted returns, on the vertical. Again, better results are in the upper left, worse in the lower right.

Furthermore, correlations between the alts classes are low. Do you recall the high correlations between traditional asset classes? (See *Figure 12: Correlations Between Traditional Asset Classes Post-GFC*, p. 53.) In contrast, look at the chart below. Alts classes have been able to maintain low correlations, making it possible to build a highly uncorrelated portfolio.

As you have learned, lower correlation means a "free lunch" of lower overall volatility, which powers compounding.

Better Tax Advantages

In the public markets, nearly all the companies are C corporations, which strips away all tax advantages from investors. In contrast, most private alts are LLCs, which pass them through to the investors.

Private Alts Correlations

	Real Estate	Private Credit	Private Equity	Venture Capital	Hedge Funds	Natural Resources	Infrastructure	S&P 500
Real Estate		0.43	0.56	0.36	0.30	0.46	0.50	0.25
Private Credit	0.43		0.77		0.82	0.53	0.13	0.66
Private Equity	0.56	0.77		0.77	0.70	0.64	0.28	0.74
Venture Capital	0.36	0.49	0.77		0.45	0.29	0.18	0.51
Hedge Funds	0.30	0.82	0.70	0.45		0.50	-0.03	0.75
Natural Resources	0.46	0.53	0.64	0.29	0.50		0.42	0.42
Infrastructure	0.50	0.13	0.28	0.18	-0.03	0.42		0.09
S&P 500	0.25	0.66	0.74	0.51	0.75	0.42	0.09	

Source: Preqin, Credit Suisse.2000-2023, Infrastructure Data from 12/31/2007

Figure 19: Private Alts Correlations

This opens the door to a wealth of tax-advantaged strategies—depreciation, depletion, and 1031 exchanges, to name a few.

We'll cover these and more in chapter 13, "How Billionaires Beat the Tax Man."

Data Driven

One of my favorite aspects of private alts is that they can be highly data-driven and predictable. Good operators can sometimes forecast revenues and expenses with accuracy and estimate returns and distributions. I love seeing the sponsor's projections, then watching the performance and how it compares.

As a case study, let's compare two income-generating mortgage REITs, one public and one private. A mortgage REIT is a pool of residential mortgages—instead of owning properties, it owns loans. NLY is a large public company. In figure 20, the dark line is the yield and the dotted line its share price. It is high yielding but has had multiple huge drawdowns, including a crash of over 65 percent. Over the term of the chart, its price has dropped from about 45 to 19, losing over half its value.

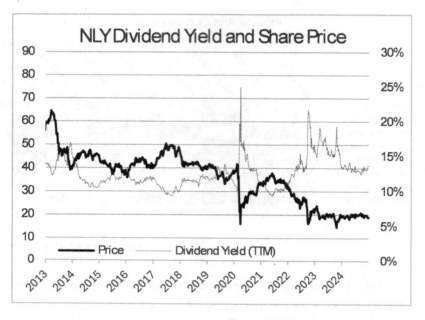

Figure 20: NLY Dividend Yield and Share Price

Compare this to our own firm's much smaller private mortgage REIT. Figure 21 shows its performance over roughly the same time period. The

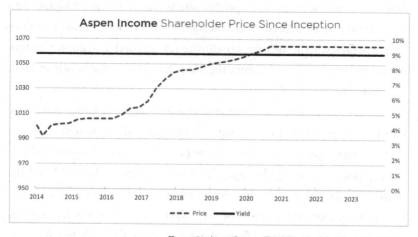

Figure 21: Aspen Income Fund Dividend Yield and Share Price

solid line is the dividend yield, and the dashed line is the share price. Its dividend yield hasn't changed, and its share price has only gone up.

Imagine trying to plan an income strategy with NLY's roller-coaster share price and wildly fluctuating dividend yield. Any poor schmuck owning it probably would have pulled their hair out. The Aspen Income Fund is easy to predict and plan. And lest you think I am unfairly comparing apples and oranges, the Aspen Income Fund is audited, does have liquidity on a quarterly basis by request, and has never failed to meet a liquidity request. It is also essentially unlevered, while NLY is levered 9:1 (for every dollar of investment, they have $9 of debt).

Higher Cash Flows

Another area where private alts can stand out is cash flow. In the public markets, it is very difficult to find stocks with consistent high-dividend payouts and little volatility. However, in the private markets, with private credit funds in particular, it is quite doable.

For retirees or endowments that need consistent high cash flows with minimal volatility, this would be life changing. I am on the board of a school operating an endowment and was speaking to a large wealth management firm about our need to produce double-digit cash flow without volatility. They stared at me speechless—I'm sure thinking I was ignorant and unrealistic. I understand why. In the public markets, it's nearly impossible, but with a few private credit funds, we were able to generate the needed double-digit income with liquidity.

THE DOWNSIDE OF ALTS

So, private alts should be a cornerstone of your investment strategy, as they are with billionaires. But alts also come with their own set of challenges to navigate. Let's look at a few of them.

Liquidity. Foremost in investors' minds is, of course, liquidity. Can you get out of your investment when you need to? In the public markets, an exit is as easy as the click of a button. In private alts, liquidity is rare. Most investments will lock up your cash for three, five, or even ten years. However, as we have mentioned, most investors overestimate their need for liquidity. It is very important you calculate your true liquidity need and manage it—which we will show you how to do in detail in chapter 15.

Sponsor Selection. Much more so than in the public markets, sponsor selection is paramount. Performance varies far more widely among private sponsors than public. This puts a greater burden on you, the investor, to select your sponsors, but the reward is there when you do. This is one way you can differentiate yourself as an investor. We will cover sponsor selection in depth in chapter 16, "How to Select an Operator."

Transparency. I will list transparency here as a negative of alts, but I don't think private alts are necessarily opaque or that public companies are very transparent. Most of the time when I read a public company's annual report, I can't find much of the data I am interested in—like revenue or expense breakdowns by product or service type, charts of daily active users over time for social media companies, the cost of battery warranties for electric vehicle companies, net asset value per share for REITs, and so on. It can be very difficult to determine their strategy.

Private alts can be quite transparent, with clear communications and reports, or they can also be very opaque, depending on the sponsor. We encourage you to avoid sponsors lacking transparency—there are too many great private sponsors out there.

All public companies are audited, as are most of the larger private alts, though few of the smaller alts are.

Complex Taxation. As we mentioned, LLCs pass on significant tax advantages to investors. The downside is that you might receive K-1s for multiple states, requiring you to file your personal tax return in each state listed. K-1s frequently arrive late, requiring you to file extensions. And if you are investing with an IRA or nonprofit, you might be subject to unrelated business taxable income (UBTI). Make sure you talk to your tax professional prior to investing.

Unregistered / Unregulated. All public companies are registered with the SEC, and with that comes regulation. That said, most of the regulations do little to protect investors and are very burdensome to the companies. Private alts are unregistered and hence unregulated. But unregulated does not mean much; alts must still comply with all federal and state laws.

And like so many of the negatives, being unregistered and unregulated can be a great positive as well. This can mean more flexibility in the investment approach, and time and cost savings. The millions of dollars spent annually on registration and regulatory compliance instead go to you, the investor.

Criticism of the Yale Model

In the Great Financial Crisis, Yale suffered significant losses, and many criticized Swensen and the Yale Model. An article in *Barron's* headlined "Crash Course" particularly stung Swensen. It criticized Yale and others for being too aggressive, too overinvested in alts, and too underinvested in stocks and bonds.[33] The article noted that private equity, real estate, oil and gas, and timber were all down, and estimated that Yale had lost about 25 percent. It was written in the middle of the crisis, before the panic had reached its bottom. At first blush, the article seems ridiculous, given that the S&P 500 did even worse, dropping 48 percent in the GFC. In a guest lecture, Swensen gave a masterful response to the criticisms:

> Let's just look at the last decade in Yale's portfolio. Over the 10 years ended June 30, 2010, domestic equities produced returns of negative 0.7% per year, bonds produced returns of 5.9% per year. Let's look at the alternatives, as opposed to domestic marketable securities. Private equity, 6.2% per year, real estate, 6.9% per year,

absolute return, 11.1% per year; timber, 12.1% per year, and oil and gas, 24.7% per year. I think the numbers speak for themselves.[34]

He concluded that the Barron article "really took far too short a time horizon."[35] Similar criticisms have continued. Critics argue that since the GFC, alts no longer have an advantage over public markets. They also argue that many peers using the Yale model underperform Yale. One article quotes a financial advisor saying investors shouldn't consider alts if they have less than $10 million, and those who do so "are endangering their retirement by gambling in the alternative-asset market."[36] I fail to see the similarity between buying an apartment complex and taking your nest egg to Las Vegas. This type of narrow thinking is typical of financial advisors who serve their own interests by playing to investors' fears.

Alts' high fees are a common criticism, but I fail to see the relevance since returns are always calculated net of fees.

Another common criticism of alts is that their true volatility is understated, or "smoothed," because private investments report their valuations quarterly, while public markets are priced daily. This is a valid concern. Many analysts use algorithms to attempt to "unsmooth" private returns, but these algorithms are suspect. A more common-sense approach is to simply smooth public market data by using only quarterly pricing. All the public market performance data presented in section 2 of this book has been smoothed by measuring only end-of-quarter valuations.

Others have claimed that alts' volatility is between 11–24 percent, that they are 93 percent correlated with US Equities, that they are not diversified, and that since the GFC, alts have underperformed traditional investments.[37] Data from multiple providers refute these claims, as do the results.

The years 2023 and 2024 saw historic returns for US equities, roughly 25 percent per year, while alts' returns were dismal. Yale reported a 5.7

percent return for the year ended June 30, 2024. However, over a longer time frame, the model's outperformance is intact. According to Yale's reports: "Yale's result exceeds that of a typical 70/30 stock and bond portfolio by 3.8 percent over both the past 10 and 20 years."[38] In these recent criticisms, I come to Swensen's same conclusion: Critics are looking at "far too short a time horizon."

THE ALTS CONTINUUM

We have learned some of the power of private alts, and soon we are going to dive deep into the particulars. But how should you get started?

Maybe, like David Swensen, you started with a $1.3 billion portfolio—but probably not! Here's how most individual investors get into alts: They start with the simpler, more approachable options, and as their investable assets and experience grow, they migrate to the more sophisticated options. We call it the *Alternative Investment Continuum*.

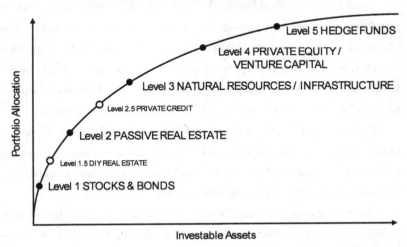

Figure 22: The Alternative Investment Continuum

Think of the Alts Continuum not as a rule or even best practices, but just as how most investors progress on their alts journey. Let's take a closer look at each level.

Level 1—Stocks and Bonds. Most folks start their investment journey as high earners or business owners. With limited knowledge of alternatives, and perhaps being nonaccredited, they jump first into stocks and bonds. Few individuals do well unless they get help from professional advisors or investor groups.

Level 1.5—DIY Real Estate. Investors may soon encounter the need for investment income, or they tire of the volatility of the public markets, or they become aware of the success of real estate investors. Andrew Carnegie is said to have remarked that "90 percent of all millionaires become so through owning real estate." While that's undoubtedly an exaggeration, real estate has produced a lot of wealth.

Some buy long-term rental homes, short-term rentals, or try their hand at housing fix-and-flip. Some may get into apartment complexes, maybe with a friend.

Level 2—Passive Real Estate. As investable assets grow, many find it's too difficult to scale and manage disparate real estate investments. You may realize that you are not doing a great job of managing the properties, or you have difficulty finding good deals to buy, or can't get good debt terms, or that there might be better opportunities in other asset classes—maybe like industrial real estatethat you don't know enough about.

Either way, the next step is typically passive real estate. It's understandable, has tax advantages, and can yield great returns. Partnering with a professional sponsor, you find properties that are well selected and well managed, taking all the pressure off you.

Passive real estate is usually the first passive asset class for high-net-worth investors. There are so many diverse and compelling options that many never go further. Passive real estate has two superpowers: inflation performance and tax benefits. We'll do a deep dive on those next in chapter 6.

Level 2.5—Private Credit. As your real estate equity grows, you might realize that you are carrying a lot of equity risk in your portfolio. You might also need additional income that real estate—especially value-add strategies—does not provide. To take advantage of many of the best tax strategies, you will also need income.

Private credit is a logical next step. These funds lend against real estate or to businesses (or other types of lending), typically at high interest rates. As lenders, they are senior to all equity investors, making the investment much safer. I find the more sophisticated the investor, the more they love debt investments. It's not uncommon to find private credit investments yielding high single digits to low teens. Private credit has a superpower: high cash flows with lower risk, perfect for income generation. We'll look in depth at private credit investments in chapter 7.

Level 3—Natural Resources / Infrastructure. The most uncorrelated asset classes of all are natural resources and infrastructure. They also can generate strong cash flow, tax advantages, and carry lower risk. We'll cover these more in chapter 11.

Level 4—Private Equity / Venture Capital. Everyone has heard about the guy who invested in the "unicorn" stock before its IPO and got rich. Others know that operating businesses can have higher returns than real estate, or that private equity is a huge space with a great track record of returns. Others are just looking for diversification from real estate.

Either way, private equity has a strong track record and lots of appealing options. Its superpower is having the highest risk-adjusted returns of any asset class. We'll go in depth on these in chapter 8, "Private Equity," and chapter 9, "Venture Capital."

Level 5—Hedge Funds / Other. More sophisticated and deeper-pocketed investors sometimes are intrigued by celebrity investor-savants running hedge funds or enamored with exotic and brilliant money-making strategies like arbitrage, or long-short. Others are looking for a source of more uncorrelated returns.

Hedge funds can outperform the market at times and underperform at others. A hedge fund's superpower is in delivering returns similar to those of public markets, but with lower volatility. We'll do a deep dive in chapter 10 "Hedge Funds" and look at a few other asset classes in chapter 11 "Other Alternatives."

At this point, you are probably itching to get into the details of private alts. In the next section, we will do just that in each of our alts asset classes.

PART 2

DEEP DIVE: PRIVATE ALTS

In this section we will begin looking at private alts in depth. Our goal here is to help you learn about the various alts classes—what they are, their unique superpowers, and how they perform in various economic climates.

The markets typically have long periods of gains punctuated by brief crashes. Three recent crashes were the dot-com crash, the Great Financial Crisis, and COVID, which lasted approximately 1.75, 1.5, and 0.25 years, respectively. The subsequent boom periods were much more extended, lasting 5, 10.75, and 4.25 years.

Throughout this section, I will present detailed performance data. I will generally not share linear data, because the start and end dates materially change the total returns. I prefer to separate the total drawdown in crash periods to show the risk sensitivity of the classes, and the annualized returns during the boom periods to show normal performance.

Figure 23 illustrates alts classes in three recent market crashes.

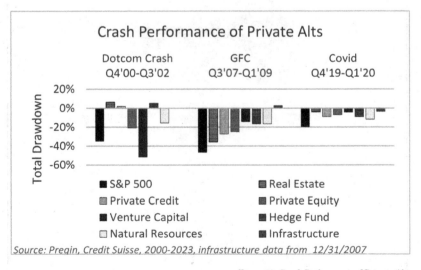

Figure 23: Crash Performance of Private Alts

In the dot-com crash, venture capital suffered, and in the Great Financial Crisis, real estate took a big hit. But in all other cases, alts experienced much more limited drawdowns.

This is very important because, as we have learned, in the battle of investing, limiting losses is far more important than maximizing gains.

So, alts limit the downside, but what about the upside? Figure 24 shows how our alts classes performed in the booms between.

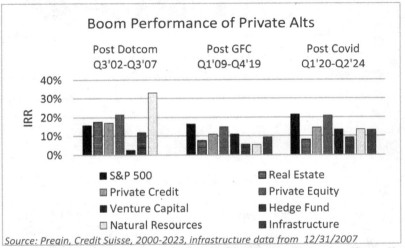

Figure 24: Boom Performance of Private Alts

In the post–dot-com boom, alts outperformed, except for venture capital. In the others, the alts classes performed well but slightly lagged the S&P 500.

Again, coming back to the idea of *risk-adjusted* returns, figures 26 and 27 show different measures of return relative to the risk. In this case, risk is defined as variance of return. The more volatile the returns, the riskier the investment. You can see that every alts class has lower risk than the S&P 500, and many yield the same or higher returns.

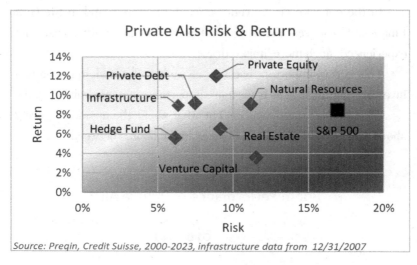

Figure 25: Private Alts Risk and Return

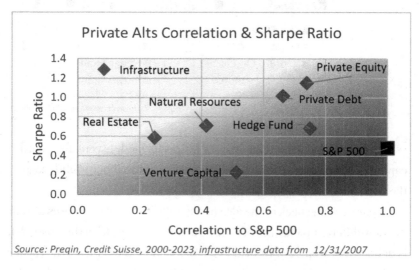

Figure 26: Private Alts S&P 500 Correlation and Sharpe Ratio

Before we continue, a few words about historical performance data:
- The charts above are *indexes*, which show *averages*. This means that many alts performed much better, and many performed much worse (recall our dispersion chart, p. 71).
- All historical data suffers from *survivor bias*, whereby failed funds disappear from the data, skewing the results upward.
- Most index data is obtained via surveys, with the possibility that poor performance is underreported, which is called *selection bias*. These last two biases are mitigated by the methodologies employed by top data providers.
- Our alts classes combine highly disparate things, and again, averages hide the full story. Real estate combines office, retail, and multifamily sectors, which are very different; hedge funds combine twelve strategies that are wildly unrelated.

These are all reasons not to rely on simplistic charts as your primary decision-making tool, but instead use them to provide context as you learn about these amazing asset classes.

Now we will jump into our Alts Continuum deep dive—and first up is real estate. Let's go!

CHAPTER 6

PRIVATE REAL ESTATE

"Don't wait to buy real estate. Buy real estate and wait."
- **Will Rogers**

In this chapter, we will unpack commercial real estate—likely your first private investment. We will look at its advantages and disadvantages, breaking down the different sectors, their strengths and weaknesses, and the best times to buy.

ADVANTAGES OF PRIVATE REAL ESTATE
There are a lot of things to love about real estate.
- **Inflation Performance.** Real estate is one of the best ways to beat inflation; real estate rents consistently match inflation. And that's just the income. You also benefit from appreciation, and the fact that real estate is easily leveraged means you multiply the inflation benefit three to four times. And it doesn't end there—remember our discussion about inflation being another way to tap the miracle of compounding (p. 35)? The value of your debt decreases from inflation too. That's three inflation levers—and why this is one of real estate's superpowers.

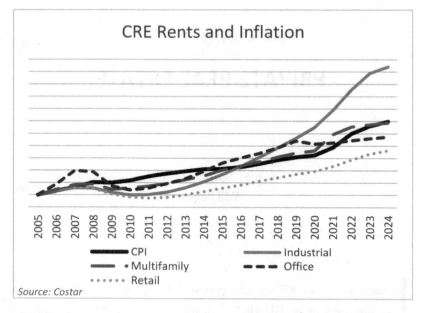

Figure 27: Real Estate Income and Inflation

- **Tax Benefits.** Private real estate is replete with tax benefits—its second superpower. We'll cover them in chapter 13.
- **Negative Correlation to Stocks.** By now, you know the billionaire's core investment strategy: Reduce volatility by uncorrelated investment. Private real estate is one of the best ways to achieve low correlations: -0.3 according to J.P. Morgan[39] and 0.25 according to Preqin.
- **Excellent Risk-Adjusted Returns.** Good sponsors have been able to beat market returns (see *Figure 18: Public and Private Manager Dispersion*, p. 71).
- **High Cash Flows.** Some private real estate investments have abundant cash flow, making them suitable for income generation.

Drawbacks

The drawbacks of private real estate investments are the same ones listed in the previous chapter that are common to all alts: liquidity, transparency, sponsor selection, and being unregistered/unregulated.

WHY PRIVATE REAL ESTATE VS. PUBLIC REITS?

Public REITs are very popular. Given the advantages of real estate, why not just buy REITs? There are numerous reasons.

REITs Are Highly Correlated to the Stock Market. This factor alone is enough to keep the ultrawealthy away. The billionaire's first principle is to enhance compounding by reducing volatility through an uncorrelated portfolio. Over four decades, REITs have had a 0.6 correlation to the stock market, but more recently, it is closer to 0.9—extremely high. During the same period, raw real estate had a -0.1 correlation.[40]

Volatility. Along the same line, REITs share the volatility of the stock market. Figure 28 shows the premium or discount paid by REIT investors relative to the value of the real estate.

REITs Cannot Access Value-Add Strategies. In order to avoid double taxation, REITs are required to distribute 90 percent of their income to investors. This means they cannot use cash to improve or develop properties, some of the most lucrative real estate strategies. We invested in a medical office building purchased from a REIT for $6.9 million. They paid $19 million 6 years earlier. It was an older building that needed major renovations, and the REIT couldn't afford to invest that much because of their distribution requirements.

Limited Tax Benefits. While REITs avoid 90 percent of double taxation, they cannot pass on to investors many tax benefits like 1031 exchanges, depreciation, or Opportunity Zones.

REITs Rely on Short-Term Debt Structures. REITs rely primarily on short-term corporate debt for funding rather than long-term debt. This puts them more at risk from interest rates volatility.

OVERVIEW OF REAL ESTATE SECTORS

Multifamily. Apartments consistently have the lowest cap rates of all real estate sectors. Apartments are the gold standard of real estate and are considered the safest sector, since people always need a place to live.

Office. Office has historically had the next most favorable cap rates, but since 2015, it has become the worst.

Retail and Industrial. Retail and industrial have similar cap rates.

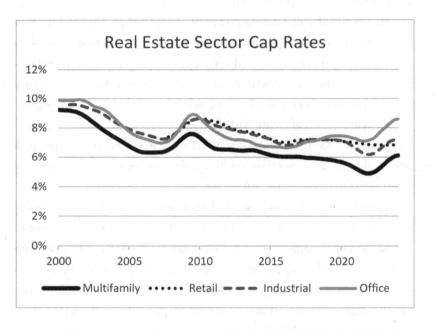

Figure 29: Real Estate Cap Rates by Sector

WHAT IS A CAP RATE?

A cap rate, or capitalization rate, is the primary method for valuing commercial real estate. This is an important metric to understand, but it's not as complicated as you might think.

Real estate produces net operating income (income after operating expenses, called NOI), which becomes the primary basis for valuing the property. NOI will be divided by the cap rate to determine the property's value.

As an example, if a property produces $100,000 in NOI and the cap rate is 5 percent, that property would be worth $2 million. If the is 10 percent, that property would be worth $1 million.

It's important to note that cap rate are inversely correlated to a property's value. Meaning, the lower the cap rate, the more valuable the property, and vice versa.

ECONOMIC DRIVERS OF REAL ESTATE

Real estate values are driven primarily by a blend of three economic factors.

Interest Rates. Real estate competes with other yield-driven investments and thus values track with bonds. The chart below shows ten-year Treasury rates.

Economic Strength. Real estate values are dependent upon income, which is sensitive to overall economic strength. The chart below shows inverse economic strength as negative GDP growth.

Inflation. Because real estate is a top inflation hedge, inflation increases values. The chart below shows inverse inflation as negative PCE.

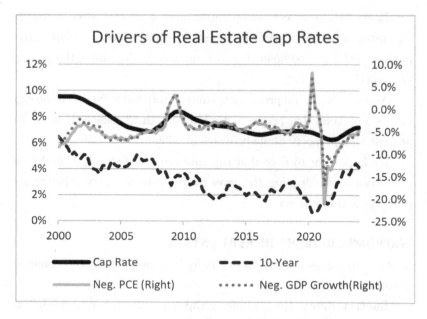

Figure 30: Economic Drivers of Real Estate Cap Rates

You can see each of these factors "pulling" on cap rates in the chart. Notice the black line—real estate cap rates is being influenced by the three factors, in gray.

RECESSION PERFORMANCE

All real estate is sensitive to recession, some sectors more than others. The chart below shows the change in vacancy rates by sector through two recent recessions.

Multifamily. Apartments are more stable in recession because people always need a place to live, in good times and bad.

Retail. Retail is more sensitive to recession because, in difficult times, people will prioritize rent over shopping. However, some shopping is always a must—like groceries, drugs, hardware for repair—so retail is more resilient than other sectors.

PRIVATE REAL ESTATE 99

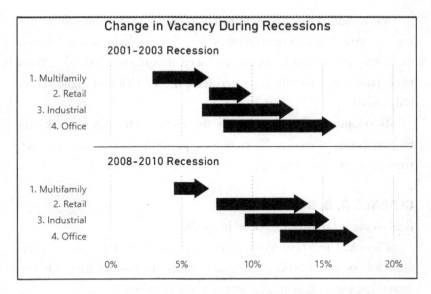

Figure 31: Vacancy Rates: Recession Performance of Real Estate Sectors

Industrial. Industrial real estate is next in sensitivity to recession, since businesses will slow expansion during difficult times.

Office. Office is most sensitive to recession.

STRATEGIES

Operators have several options in terms of investment strategies. These strategies apply to every sector. Here are the most common, in order of increasing effort, risk, and return.

Core. Core real estate is very low-risk, stable properties with long-term leases and little or no maintenance or upgrades required. These properties are generally newer buildings located in prime locations within large metropolitan markets.

Core Plus. Core plus real estate requires more effort from the operator, which might include light upgrades, improving tenant quality, and finding management efficiencies.

Value-Add. Value-add real estate requires significant effort from the operator. These properties may have low occupancy, management problems, deferred maintenance, and need of significant upgrades. These properties are generally older and have higher risk and higher potential reward.

Development. Development is the riskiest strategy but also the highest potential return. Risks include permitting, cost and time overruns, and unknown demand.

CLASSES A, B, C

Real estate is typically classified by quality.

Class A. These properties are newer (typically less than fifteen years old), little deferred maintenance, and feature the best location, the best amenities, the highest-quality tenants, and the highest rents.

Vacancy rates tend to run higher in Class A properties, reflecting their higher cost.

Class A properties are more subject to economic strength and weakness, booming in a strong economy as renters upgrade their lifestyles, and suffering in a slow economy, as people opt to step down in class.

Most new developments tend to be in Class A, which can result in oversupply and absorption issues when the economy softens.

Class B. These are one step lower in quality, generally ten to twenty years old.

Class C. These are also generally older (twenty-plus years), command the lowest rents, and are of the lowest quality in terms of deferred maintenance, location, amenities, and tenant quality. In multifamily, Class C properties are considered "workforce housing." In good economic times, these properties lag, as renters choose upgraded properties; Class C tends to do better in poor economic times as renters choose cheaper options.

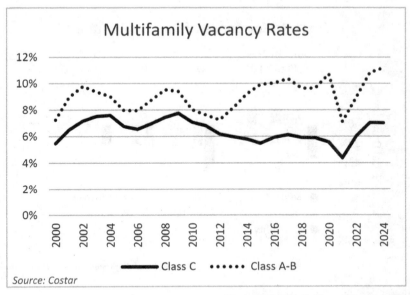

Figure 32: Multifamily Vacancy Rates by Class

RISK AND RETURN

You might be interested to see how the various real estate sectors perform in boom and recession, as well as their correlation to the S&P 500. Some important caveats here though:

- The charts below do not show fund performance like the charts in other chapters, but raw, unlevered real estate prices. Income, expenses, and fees are not included, so these charts cannot be compared to the similar charts elsewhere in this book.
- The data in these charts come from "equal-weighted" indexes, which count large and small transactions equally. Value-weighted indexes show much more volatility, reflecting the fact that large properties experience both steeper appreciation and declines.

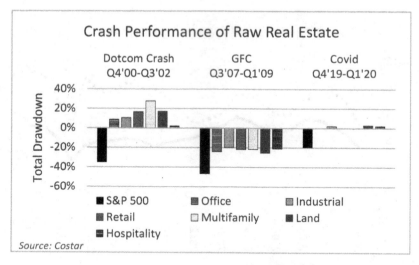

Figure 33: Crash Performance of Raw Real Estate

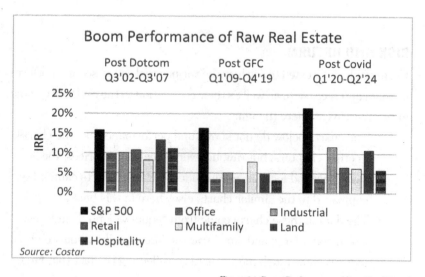

Figure 34: Boom Performance of Raw Real Estate

PRIVATE REAL ESTATE   103

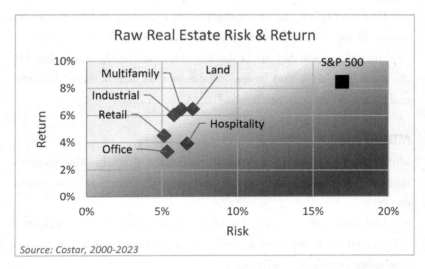

Figure 35: Raw Real Estate Risk & Return

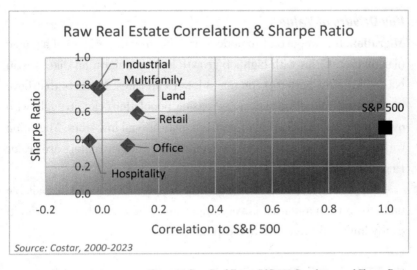

Figure 36: Raw Real Estate S&P 500 Correlation and Sharpe Ratio

Real estate performed exceptionally well in both up and down markets, except for the Great Financial Crisis and its aftermath.

You can also see that raw real estate values are highly uncorrelated to the public markets—and far less volatile as well. Again, these show raw real estate values only, not income.

MULTIFAMILY

Multifamily is the largest commercial real estate sector, has the strongest recession resilience of all sectors, and generally commands the lowest cap rates.

Multifamily also has the highest depreciation of any commercial real estate, making it the most favorable if you are using many of the tax strategies we will lay out in chapter 13.

Here are a few things to consider when evaluating an investment in multifamily:

Key Drivers of Value

Migration. It is important to understand the growth (or lack) of a particular market. Cities with high job growth and net migration (like Austin, Nashville, and Charlotte) command lower cap rates. Markets that have net negative migration (i.e., a decreasing population) can struggle with oversupply and a lack of interest from institutional investors. Migration within cities is also important to evaluate (e.g., whether renters are preferring urban or suburban areas).

Supply and Demand. Looking at the supply and demand of available units for rent in a market is very important. These numbers can significantly impact rent growth and cap rates.

> Supply and demand can significantly impact rent growth and cap rates.

Supply. It's important to understand the total population of renters in a market relative to the available supply (and projected supply) of rentable units. Many sponsors try to forecast the amount of new supply being delivered to a market and the expected time it will take to absorb those new units. In high-growth markets, there can be a lot of new units under development, but the hope is that future population growth will absorb that supply. Excess supply in a market creates more competition and can result in flat or negative rent growth. Supply-constrained markets generally will be less volatile and have more consistent rent growth.

Demand. Forecasting the demand for rental units can be more difficult, as you must consider several factors, including population growth, household formation, lifestyle changes, and relative costs of a mortgage. It is usually fairly easy to find historical population growth numbers in a market, which can be helpful in assessing future expectations. Household formation is less linear and is the rate at which new households are formed (through marriage or partners living together). When households form, they generally want to upgrade their living situation (move out of their parents' house, move into a bigger apartment, or buy their first house). In recent decades, a delay in household formation has kept a larger population of renters. Additionally, with single-family housing continuing to price out many first-time homebuyers, the renter population is likely to remain large.

Key Risks

NOI Growth Potential. In most acquisitions of multifamily—whether it's core plus, value-add, or development—the sponsor group generally expects net operating income (NOI) to grow over time. Evaluating the assumptions on what is driving that growth and the likelihood of achieving it are paramount to determining if the property will sell for a higher value down the road. When looking at pro forma rent assumptions, it's important to look at comparable properties within a few-mile radius to see what other similar properties are achieving for the same level of amenities and finish. The potential rent of a property becomes the ceiling on how much revenue a property can generate, so it's very important to get this right. The other area sponsors generally try to improve NOI is decreasing expenses. While this can be done, it is generally very difficult to achieve meaningful results, especially since maintenance expenses only grows as properties age.

Cap Ex Risk. If the sponsor group expects to achieve a higher NOI, they generally will need to spend money on capital expenditures to do so. This can include adding amenities to the property or improving the units with nicer finishes. The larger the cap ex budget, the larger the risk. The biggest risks come from underbudgeting how much certain items will cost and running out of money. Another risk is that after spending money on those items, they don't actually translate to being able to charge higher rents.

Absorption Risk. This was touched on earlier in the supply and demand section, but absorption risk is sometimes an under weighted risk. Many times, when taking on a value-add project, the property may not cash flow for a period of time during the renovation, and certain assumptions are made about how quickly those units will get leased (absorbed). But in high-supply markets (or submarkets), it can be challenging to do. Higher supply puts pressure both on time frames to lease and lease rates. If a project doesn't cash flow during the renovation period, then the interest-carry cost can weigh down a project and potentially eat into cash reserves intended for something else.

Tenancy Risk. Another factor not always considered in multifamily is the quality of the expected tenant base. This is usually driven by the Class (A, B, or C) of the property. It is important to make sure the assumptions in the pro forma match the tenant base. Class C properties generally attract lower-income households, and it is usually expected that collections and bad debt will be issues. Additionally, if the renter base relies on government assistance, that needs to be factored in.

On the other hand, a Class A property may have a tenant base with stronger household incomes, but it is important to ensure that the pro forma rents are in line with the median area income. Otherwise, it may be difficult to lease the property up since your rental rates will be leading the market.

The factors to consider also include market risk, operator risk, debt risks, etc., but the above cover the big areas to start your evaluation.

Other Things to Consider

Class A, B, C Pros and Cons. Class A properties typically have less deferred maintenance, offer newer amenities, and will attract stronger tenants. However, Class A properties will also command the lowest cap rates (i.e., highest values) and are likely to produce lower returns. They can also experience higher vacancy during recessions as tenants move to more affordable properties.

Class C properties often have more deferred maintenance, less attractive amenities, and usually attract a weaker tenant base. However, because they require significant operational expertise, they can offer potential upside through property renovation and expense optimization. These activities can produce positive outcomes in the net operating income, which can increase the value. But as mentioned earlier, these types of properties carry inherently more risk.

Class B properties sit somewhere in the middle of the above from a risk/return standpoint. They generally have less deferred maintenance and will be newer than Class C, but their units might need renovation, creating the opportunity to improve value.

Economic Resilience. Multifamily assets are generally considered recession-resilient, driven by the essential need for housing, which keeps demand stable during downturns.

Inflation. Short-term leases, often annual or month-to-month, provide flexibility to adjust rents during inflationary periods.

INDUSTRIAL

Industrial real estate is the second-largest commercial real estate sector, has historically been a favored asset class by institutional investors, and generally commands lower cap rates—though not as low as multifamily.

Industrial real estate has been growing over the past several decades due to the rise of e-commerce and the need for warehousing and distribution centers. It is also benefitting from the deglobalization trend, which is bringing manufacturing and supply chains back to the US.

Key Drivers of Value

Geographic Location. In industrial real estate, location plays an important role. With the rise of e-commerce, access and proximity to major markets is important for logistics- or distribution-focused properties. Coastal markets have historically been "gateway" markets because of importing goods. These markets can be affected by changes in our trade relationships with various countries. Midwest markets have generally been focused on distribution, given their access to most of the country within a one- to two-days' drive. There has also been an increase in manufacturing facilities in these areas due to access to cheaper, blue-collar labor forces.

Primary vs. Secondary Markets. There are pros and cons to investing in primary versus secondary markets. Primary markets are generally more competitive, with significant institutional capital, and tend to trade at lower cap rates. Secondary markets may be less developed but are often growth markets. If primary markets vacancy is tight, tenants will look to secondary markets. Further, as companies look to expand manufacturing operations, they may consider secondary markets because of the cheaper labor force.

Building Specifications. Understanding the needs of potential tenants in a market is very important. A building focused on distribution (or what's called cross-docking), will be designed and laid out much differently than one intended for heavy manufacturing. As such, the use case of the building determines the potential tenant base as it can be costly to convert older buildings to a different use. Therefore, sponsors need to ensure the tenant demand is there for each type of building. Additionally, older buildings were generally built with much lower ceiling heights than are now standard today.

Development vs. Existing Buildings. Similar to multifamily, there are different strategies to invest in industrial. Some sponsors look for older buildings with tenants that are paying below-market rents. The idea is to purchase the building at a good value, hold until the tenant's leases expire, and then adjust them to market rents. Other sponsors evaluate a market to develop new buildings in the hopes of attracting quality tenants. Both strategies have their benefits and drawbacks. New buildings generally command the highest rents and appeal to the highest-quality tenants; however, you generally need to build before you have leases in place (called speculative development), so you are taking absorption risk.

Key Risks

Understanding Lease Structure. In industrial real estate, the leases can be much more complicated to understand than in multifamily, which are straightforward. There are gross leases, net leases, and modified leases (which are explained below) that all have different components to them. Industrial lease terms are usually between five and ten years, much longer than multifamily. Sometimes there are annual adjustments to the lease rate to account for inflation, but in strong inflationary environments, lease rates may lag the market. Understanding the types of leases, demand for them, and what the market will absorb all go into the assumptions for an investment. If any of these are off, it can significantly impact the value of the project.

Tenancy Risk. The quality of tenants obviously impacts multifamily, but for industrial, understanding the quality of your tenants becomes paramount. In multifamily, if you have a bad tenant, you can evict and replace them; any single unit going vacant likely doesn't impact your bottom line much. However, in industrial, where you may have only a few tenants (or one), in your building, if they run into problems, it is much more impactful to the bottom line. That is why banks spend most of their focus on underwriting the tenants in a building. Having strong tenants (sometimes called "credit tenants") will impact the leverage you can obtain, as well as the cap rate at which the building will sell.

Functional Obsolescence. As mentioned above, older buildings were usually built with much lower ceiling heights. Additionally, the way the building is laid out and its primary use case (manufacturing vs. distribution) will impact its ability to secure new leases. As these properties age, they can sometimes become functionally obsolescent, which means the value becomes significantly less because structural issues make undesirable to new tenants. As business preferences and market dynamics change, over time that can negatively impact building values.

Economic and Business Cycle Reliance. Because businesses are the end users of this type of real estate, they are inherently tied to the business cycle. If the economy is doing well and businesses are expanding, that will positively impact industrial real estate. Conversely, when the economy is slow or in recession, the industrial sector can significantly slow down. Because of this, industrial real estate tends to see big swings in development based on the business cycle.

Other Things to Consider

Subcategories. There are several subcategories of different types of industrial real estate:
- **Logistics:** Abundant docking, easy access to highways and rail.
- **Flex Space:** A blend of office and light industrial functions, normally catering to small businesses needing versatile spaces.

- **Manufacturing Facilities:** Can be designed for light or heavy manufacturing, may require specialized infrastructure, and are driven by sectors like automotive and clean energy.

Lease Structures. There are also several different types of lease structures you should be familiar with.
- **NNN (Triple Net) Leases:** These are the most valuable types of lease where tenants cover the big three expenses—taxes, insurance, and maintenance—leaving landlords with minimal expenses. Properties leased to investment-grade tenants (e.g., Amazon, Walmart) act like investment-grade bonds, offering low-risk and low cap rates due to stable, predictable income.
- **Modified Gross Leases:** Landlord and tenant share some expenses, providing moderate control over costs and slightly lower margins than NNN.
- **Full-Service Gross Leases:** Landlords bear all operating costs, leading to higher expenses and lower margins, while tenants benefit from fixed costs.

Inflation. As mentioned earlier, industrial leases often include annual rent escalations, which can provide an inflation hedge. However, if inflation is strong, the leases may lag market rents until the leases expire.

RETAIL REAL ESTATE

Retail real estate is another core commercial sector and covers a wide variety of property types. Retail properties generally trade at higher cap rates than multifamily and industrial, but that largely depends on location, property type, and tenant quality.

Retail real estate has been significantly impacted over the past several decades as consumers have shifted more of their spending online. However, most retailers still pursue an omnichannel approach to reach customers (online and physical locations), and the sector has stabilized. Additionally, "retail" real estate can cover a variety of subcategories (which we'll discuss below), including malls, big-box power centers, neighborhood strip centers, and grocery-anchored centers.

> The advent of e-commerce fundamentally shifted consumer preferences.

Key Drivers of Value

Consumer Preferences. As mentioned above, the advent of e-commerce several decades ago fundamentally shifted consumer preferences. Many pundits thought the entire sector would eventually become nonexistent, but it has since stabilized as many retailers reach consumers through an omnichannel strategy. However, certain types of retail, such as malls, have struggled more than others to recover. Because retail real estate is driven by consumer preferences, it is important to understand how those preferences shift to spot opportunity. As an example, in neighborhood strip centers, many tenants provide services that can't be sold online—think dog groomers, liquor stores, cell phone retailers, etc.—and therefore are more immune to preference shifts.

Location. As with other types of real estate, location is very important for retailers; it's often the single factor that determines success. Visibility from roads/highways, accessibility, traffic flow, and parking all impact a consumer's decision to shop. Location within a market is also an important consideration. As consumer preferences change, urban versus suburban locations may be impacted differently. For example, since COVID-19 and the tidal shift of employees working from home, neighborhood strip centers located in suburban residential areas have thrived.

Supply vs. Demand. Likewise, it's important to understand the supply and demand factors within a market for the specific property type. Looking at the competition around a particular property will impact the decisions tenants make to sign leases. Because retailers are focused on consumers, researching the local demographics in a three-to-five-mile radius is critical, as this area becomes the core customer base. As with industrial, leases can be structured in a variety of ways (triple net, gross, and modified gross), so it's critical to look at other leases being signed in that market to understand what assumptions can be made in the underwriting.

Type of Retail. As mentioned before, different types of real estate all perform distinctly from each other based on shifts in consumer behavior. Malls have generally struggled to recover and in many cases have shut down. Similarly, big-box retail has struggled as many of those retailers were impacted by e-commerce growth. However, neighborhood retail has thrived in the work-from-home era with service-based tenants. And grocery-anchored retail has performed well as consumers continue to shop in person for their groceries, and that foot traffic drives tertiary visits to surrounding stores. Understanding the type of retail real estate you're investing in—and the thesis behind why the sponsor believes it will be successful—is crucial.

Key Risks

Market Risk. Retail real estate tends to be hyperlocalized, so understanding the immediate submarket is critical to the potential success or failure of an investment. Digging into the demographics of the local area—population, average age, median household income, etc.—will provide more color to the potential customer base.

Tenancy Risk. As with industrial, retail real estate also carries tenant risk. Because these tenants are businesses, looking at the strength of the individual businesses is paramount. If tenants go out of business, they can be very costly to replace, not only due to lost income, but also from spending capital on improvements to attract a new tenant. The higher the quality of the tenants, the more valuable the property will be. Similarly, the types of leases that are structured significantly impact the value of the property.

Economic and Business Cycle Reliance. Again, similar to industrial, retail real estate tenants are businesses, making these properties inherently tied to the business cycle. If the economy is doing well and consumers are spending, that will positively impact retail real estate. Conversely, when the economy is slow or in recession, the retail sector can significantly slow down.

Other Things to Consider

Subcategories of retail real estate

- **Big-Box Power Centers:** These are strip centers with usually a handful of tenants and large physical footprints—think Best Buy or Petco. Because the retailers were generally larger, many times they would be considered credit tenants (i.e., higher quality). However, e-commerce disrupted many of these businesses, and we've seen many struggle or even close down. This has impacted the vacancy of these property types.
- **Malls:** Traditional indoor malls have been significantly impacted by e-commerce, causing many to shut down altogether. Some outdoor malls and indoor malls in certain locations continue to thrive, however.
- **Neighborhood Strip Centers:** These are generally strip centers with smaller footprints located in suburban areas. The tenant base is often more local—restaurants, hair stylists, liquor stores, etc.—but can also include national credit tenants. Often these retailers are service-based and therefore have been less impacted by e-commerce.

- **Grocery-Anchored Centers:** These properties can be similar to neighborhood strip centers as they are also usually located in suburban areas, but the defining feature is the anchor tenant. Grocery stores have continued to be successful and have yet to be fully disrupted by e-commerce. And because they drive a lot of foot traffic, they're considered great anchor tenants to support surrounding tenants that benefit from spillover visits.

Inflation Considerations. Many retail leases include percentage rent clauses and CPI-based escalations, ensuring rents rise with inflation.

OTHER REAL ESTATE NICHES

We've covered three of the largest and most common real estate sectors. However, numerous smaller real estate niches can be popular investment options for syndications. For the sake of brevity, our review of these niches will be cursory.

Office. Office real estate is actually one of the largest real estate sectors, but we've decided not to do a comprehensive review as most investors will never invest in this sector. Following the fundamental shift toward remote and hybrid work, office real estate has struggled significantly. It remains to be seen how office buildings will recover and/or be converted into different uses, such as apartment buildings. However, office conversion projects generally don't pencil out. Office may become an attractive place to invest down the road, but our recommendation is to avoid investing in this sector.

Medical Office. Another niche asset class that has gained momentum in recent years is medical office. This class is much different than traditional office in that the properties are specially designed for medical groups, which often are attractive tenants. And with the aging baby boomer population, there continue to be strong tailwinds behind the sector. Often requiring significant cap ex to house medical equipment, tenant retention is generally very high. Similar to retail and industrial, the lease structure is important to understand.

Self-Storage. Another popular real estate niche is self-storage. These have become more common as more Americans stow their excess stuff. Self-storage facilities have a lot of similarities to multifamily but have less operational overhead to manage. Leases are usually structured on a month-to-month basis, and in researching supply and demand, the focus is hyper-local—usually within a five-mile radius. Drivers of demand for self-storage vary—but can be more cyclical than multifamily and track the economic cycle.

Mobile Home Parks. Once a sector scorned by investors given the stereotype, mobile home parks have become a very popular real estate niche in recent years. Driven by the need for affordable housing and the restricted supply of new parks, these can be attractive investments. There are two main types: park-owned homes and tenant-owned homes. Most investors prefer tenant-owned homes, as the responsibility of maintenance is on the tenant; these usually attract a higher-quality tenant. Attracting quality tenants can be a challenge, since these parks appeal to low-income families and therefore can be more difficult to manage.

Hotels. Hotels are a lesser-known option for investors, but this real estate nichehas been a sector many investors have had success in. Hotels can range from boutique to a national brand. Operations require specialized knowledge and training, so it's important to work with groups with a strong track record. Hotels compete with a hyper-local set of others, and the pro forma will take into account the average daily rate that can be charged, the quality (or star level) of the facility, the average occupancy, etc. Because hotels rely on travel, they can be heavily dependent on the economic cycle. In recessions or downturns, consumers and businesses cut travel from their budgets.

Land. Many long-term investors choose to invest in land. This can be lucrative, especially if the land is improved (subdivided, rezoned, entitled, etc.) and developed or sold to developers. But land is also illiquid, doesn't produce cash flow, and may not appreciate in line with inflation. For these reasons, it's important to understand local trends in demand and development.

David Swensen preferred smaller operators for his real estate investment. He shunned deals that focused on "core" stabilized assets but sought smaller, innovative firms that had a "competitive advantage, either by property type or market, and preferably a focus on an out-of-favor sector."[41]

This is a lot to chew on, no doubt. Don't feel overwhelmed by the data—just use it to form general ideas at this point—and you can always come back later to reference the specifics if needed. For now, if you're wondering where to begin, head over to investlikeabillionaire.org/book for our current recommendations.

Now let's pivot a bit into one of the best alts for income generation.

CHAPTER 7

PRIVATE CREDIT

"The borrower is servant to the lender."
- **Proverbs 22:7 (NLT) in the Bible**

I n the universe of private alts, private credit is a hidden gem and one of my favorite investment classes. Its characteristics of cash flow, safety, and liquidity make it ideal for income generation, and as such, it should be a core component of many portfolios. Private credit's superpower is high cash flows with lower risk. Billionaires tend to allocate smaller amounts here than you might, because few billionaires need investments with income or liquidity.

WHAT IS PRIVATE CREDIT?

Private credit is *lending*. While equity investors become *owners* of the investment, carrying most of the risk and the reward, credit investors become its *lenders*, with limited upside but far less risk. Often private credit is *secured*, meaning they have a claim on the assets (like real estate) to back the investment. There might also be a guarantee, meaning the investment is backed by the personal monies of the founders, executives, or other guarantors.

When lenders are secured, they have a priority claim on the assets of the business in bankruptcy or liquidation. Lenders have the first right to those assets to recover their investment, making credit investment much less risky than equity investment.

With less risk comes lower returns. With equity bets perhaps you may be able to earn 15–20 percent returns, and with credit, perhaps 8–14 percent—but with a fraction of the risk. Remember our lessons on volatility? Because minimizing losses is far more important than maximizing gains, I'll take that trade-off any day.

Let's look at a few flavors of private credit.

> Private credit's superpower is high cash flows with lower risk.

Commercial Real Estate Credit

Commercial real estate private credit is less common than other private credit but is my preferred subclass. Here are some common use cases:

- Gap funding is needed when a sponsor needs $20 million in financing above the senior loan but can raise only $15 million. Capital from a private lender is used to fill the gap.
- Bridge funding is needed when a sponsor has an approaching closing deadline, and permanent financing cannot close in time. Private credit offers a way to close the purchase, which will be replaced by permanent financing.
- Agency acquisitions GSE lenders like Fannie Mae and Freddie Mac offer permanent financing with low interest rates and attractive terms. The debt is also assumable by the new owner when the property is purchased. However, the in-place loan is often too small relative to the value of the property— more debt is needed to maximize the returns of the

investment. Private lenders can come in with an additional tranche of capital.
- Backfill financing is when a property might have very attractive in-place debt, but additional capital is needed for expansion. Rather than refinancing existing debt, private lenders can lend in second position.

Real estate private credit is the safest and lowest yielding of private credit options.

Hard Money Lending

Hard money lending, sometimes called "trust deeds" lending, is typically used for short-term fix and flip loans on residential housing. Loans are typically:
- Short term, 1–3 years
- High interest rates, 10–15 percent
- Sometimes offer interest-only payments
- Fast approval and fast closing

These funds can do well in any economic environment but can suffer in times of extreme financial duress. During the Great Financial Crisis, many hard money funds struggled to pay back investors, and some took losses. They took back properties but found prices were lower than expected and, in some cases, took properties in various stages of construction and renovation. Most of the funds, however, weathered the storm and paid investors back, albeit over a longer period of time.

Private Equity & Venture Lending

We'll cover private equity in the next chapter, but private equity sponsors buy businesses and typically borrow large sums to do so. In decades past, banks and traditional lenders provided the debt, but they have pulled back from this type of lending. Private credit has stepped in to provide the debt needed to buy the businesses or provide capital for growth.

With this kind of lending, the collateral is not real estate but the businesses being purchased or operated. Yields on private equity lending are a little higher due to the increased risk of lending against a business rather than real estate.

Cash Flow Lending

In the previous examples, the lender is secured by assets. Other private credit funds lend based on cash flows. Examples include:

- **Factoring.** These lenders finance a company's invoices. For example, Company A has a $100,000 invoice due from Company B, who is a slow payer. The private lender loans Company A $80,000 with the invoice as collateral.
- **Royalties.** Lenders may finance cash flows from royalty payments, whether mineral rights, music royalties, etc.
- **Business cash flows.** Much riskier is financing the income of the business. Venture debt is one example of this. It is often cheaper for venture capitalized companies to raise capital by pledging a portion of their cash flows rather than through traditional venture capital equity investment.

Distressed Debt

For those looking for higher-yielding opportunities, distressed debt is one of my favorites. Distressed debt funds buy troubled debt at a discount, then look for ways to maximize the value.

During 2016–2017, the debt of energy companies was selling at discounts of up to 80 percent and was secured by oil fields. Opportunistic buyers were able to double or triple their investment in twelve to eighteen months.

My own company, Aspen Funds, was able to buy non-performing residential mortgages in the aftermath of the Great Financial Crisis and generate excellent returns.

Distressed debt can be very lucrative. Performance is highly dependent upon the skill of the operator, and operator expertise and track record should be your primary area of evaluation.

One very special attribute of distressed debt is that it is *countercyclical*—it performs well when the economic cycle is at its worst. Most of your investments are pro-cyclical, mirroring the economy. I love having a portion of my portfolio that will outperform when everything else is struggling.

ADVANTAGES OF PRIVATE CREDIT

Private credit can be an excellent spot to place capital. It has a number of very appealing traits:

High Yield. Private credit funds might offer yields in the 8–14 percent range.

Cash Flow. As lenders, they receive regular payments from borrowers and usually have strong cash distributions for investors.

Liquidity. Many private credit funds have abundant internal liquidity, as their loans are paid off and offer liquidity options to investors. For example, my firm has a private credit income fund with over one thousand loans, with thirty to sixty paying off every quarter. We offer investors the ability to redeem their capital after any quarter. It has never been unable to fulfill a liquidity request so far. Such internal liquidity has limits, of course, and you should be comfortable with them.

Secured. *Secured* means they have a legal right to the assets or cash flows. Many funds have their loans secured by assets like real estate or by cash flows or other means, giving them an extra margin of safety.

These strengths make private credit a core choice for investors looking for income—a notoriously difficult thing to do in the public markets.

DISADVANTAGES OF PRIVATE CREDIT

Other things to consider:

Limited tax benefits. Most of the income received is typically interest payments and is thus taxed as ordinary income.

Market risk. Even though secured, these funds are subject to economic forces acting on the underlying assets or cash flows. But while the market risk is real, being in a debt investment has far lower risk than equity investment.

PRIORITY

It is important to understand priority when looking at private credit. Every investment has layers of capital. If you own a home, you probably have a senior mortgage lender. You may have also taken out a second mortgage and supplied a down payment as equity. Your senior lender is first priority, the second mortgage is second priority, and you are last. In a liquidation or bankruptcy, your senior lender has first claim on the value in your home. They can force a sale, and all the proceeds go to them until their debt is fully paid. Any remaining proceeds go to the second lender, until they are fully paid. Finally, as the owner, you get anything left over. This is precisely how priority works in lending.

Similarly, every investment has capital layers—called the capital stack (discussed further in chapter 19)—with the lowest being the most senior the highest being common equity. The lowest takes the least risk and has the lowest returns. The highest takes the greatest risks and has the greatest upside. The order is called the *priority* or the *position in the capital stack*. The higher layers are termed *subordinated* to the lower. Here are the positions that can exist in the capital stack, and every deal may have all or none of them.

Senior lending takes a first position in assets like real estate. Senior lenders might lend only 60–65 percent of the value of the asset and thus take very little risk. It is very rare for senior lenders to take losses, and any losses they do take are partial at worst.

Junior lending takes second position in secured assets. It is obviously riskier, but if done well, it can carry very low risk and earn higher returns.

Mezzanine lending may be secured or unsecured but is subordinated to secured debt. When secured, mezzanine debt is usually indirectly secured, not tied directly to the assets themselves but guaranteed by the entity holding the assets.

Preferred equity is technically equity but has many debt-like characteristics. Preferred equity may have the right to force a sale, may have priority rights to cash flows, and may have performance covenants related to operations.

Common equity is the final layer of capital, capturing most of the upside but also bearing most of the risk. Most lenders construct deals they believe will collect what they are owed in all but the most extreme circumstances, shifting most of the risk onto the equity owners.

PERFORMANCE

Remember that historical analysis is biased by survivorship and selection and shows only averages, which means many deals did far better and others far worse. It also lumps together the very different types of private credit. That said, here is how private credit funds performed in three recent crashes and subsequent booms.

As you can see, private credit experienced gains in the first crash, more limited drawdowns than the public markets in the other two, and averaged double-digit returns during growth periods.

Private credit has superior risk and return characteristics, as well as low correlations compared to the public markets (the upper-left corner is optimal).

One rather interesting finding is that mezzanine debt had less volatility risk than other types of private credit.

Private credit far outpaced the public markets in every metric—higher returns, lower risk, higher Sharpe ratio risk-adjusted returns, and low correlations. You can see why, in recent years, private credit has become one of the hottest areas of private alternatives.

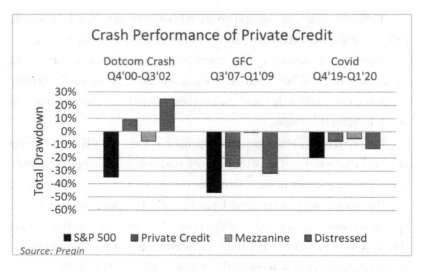

Figure 37: Crash Performance of Private Credit

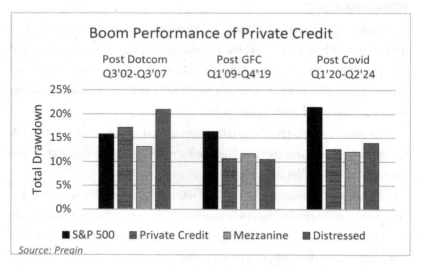

Figure 38: Boom Performance of Private Credit

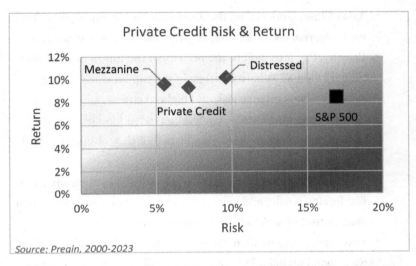

Figure 39: Private Credit Risk & Return

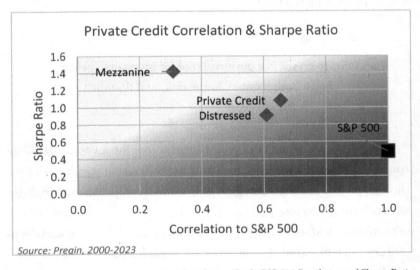

Figure 40: Private Credit S&P 500 Correlation and Sharpe Ratio

EVALUATING PRIVATE CREDIT

When evaluating private credit, follow all the principles laid out in "How to Select an Operator" (chapter 16), as well as these important factors:

- **Asset Class.** Understand the asset class being lent against. For example, real estate lending is safer than business lending.
- **Priority.** Pay attention to the priority of the fund's investments. Senior? Junior? Where are they in the capital stack? Lower priority means greater risk and higher returns.
- **Security and guarantees.** Understand what kind of security they obtain—such as liens—and whether they obtain personal guarantees.
- **Rights and covenants.** Find out what rights they typically carry, like forcing a sale; and covenants, like minimum cash flows and valuations, below which trigger protective actions.
- **Leverage.** Some funds make use of leverage, borrowing against their loan portfolio. This can dramatically increase risk, especially at higher levels.

> **Private credit is a powerful tool for investors seeking consistent income, lower risk, and liquidity.**

Private credit stands out as a powerful tool for investors seeking consistent income, lower risk, and liquidity. By offering steady cash flow through private lending strategies, it provides a compelling way to diversify and strengthen your portfolio. If you're ready to explore private credit opportunities and see our latest recommendations, visit investlikeabillionaire.org/book for up-to-date insights and expert-vetted strategies.

But private credit is just one piece of the alternative investing puzzle. Next, we'll dive into private equity, an asset class that goes beyond lending to provide ownership in high-growth businesses—offering even greater potential for outsized returns.

Let's take a closer look at why the world's wealthiest investors use private equity to build generational wealth.

CHAPTER 8

PRIVATE EQUITY

"Private equity has the unique ability to act without constraints in pursuing long-term value creation."
- Stephen A. Schwarzman

Now we come to the "granddaddy" of private alts—private equity (PE). PE has the highest alts allocation for the ultrawealthy: over 30 percent of their portfolio with over $6 trillion in assets. PE's superpower is holding the title of the highest risk-adjusted returns of any alts asset class. From the CFA Institute:

> Private equity's appeal is obvious. It has generated high returns along with low volatility, which results in high risk-adjusted returns. But the volatility of the US Private Equity index was almost 50% lower than the S&P 500's and even below that of the 10-year US government bond.[42]

PERFORMANCE
During the recent market crashes, PE exhibited far lower drawdowns and, in the subsequent booms, returns close to or exceeding the public markets.

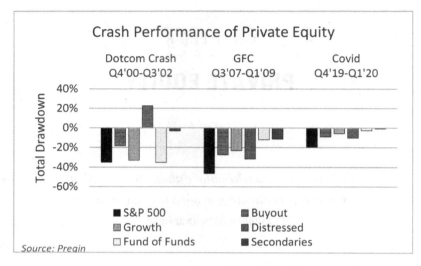

Figure 41: Crash Performance of Private Equity

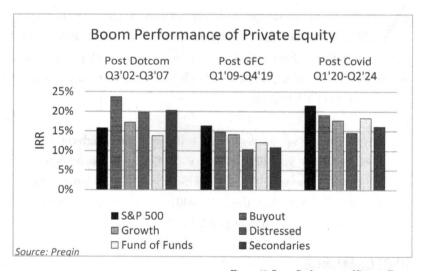

Figure 42: Boom Performance of Private Equity

PE risk and return and correlation to the public markets were also superior (upper-left corner is optimal).

PRIVATE EQUITY   133

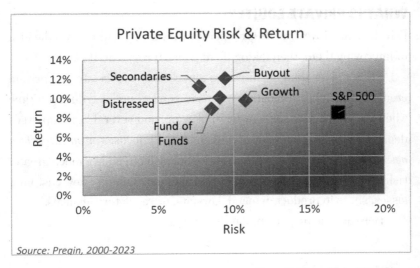

Figure 43: Private Equity Risk & Return

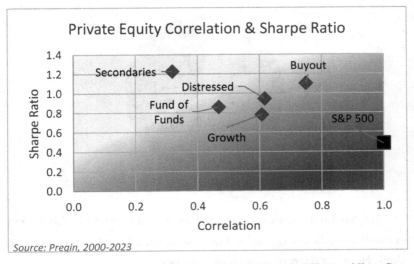

Figure 44: Private Equity Correlation to S&P 500 and Sharpe Ratio

Again, recognize that the charts show averages; many deals did much better and others much worse.

WHAT IS PRIVATE EQUITY?

Private equity investments buy operating businesses, often with the idea of improving them, then taking them public through an IPO.

PE is riskier than our first two alts classes, real estate and private credit. I remember evaluating a private equity purchase during a time when the entire management team blew up, and several key employees departed, crushing the value of the company. PE focuses on *operating businesses*, which can make greater profits but also often have much greater risks: key employee departures, management failures, key customer losses, shifts in product demand, lawsuits, or regulatory changes.

Here are the most common PE strategies:

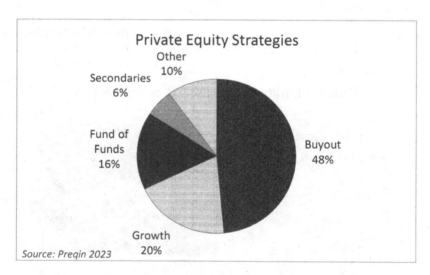

Buyout funds, sometimes called leveraged buyouts or LBOs, buy controlling stakes in operating businesses, usually with large debt positions. Here are a few of their characteristics:

- Private companies trade at a steep discount compared to public companies. Buying private companies at a discount then taking them public creates a lot of value for investors.

- They often bring in professional managers. Many private businesses are family-run with poor operational skills.
- Most will focus on growing the businesses through strategic partnerships forged by the sponsor.
- They also focus on reducing expenses by combining staff of multiple businesses, negotiating vendor discounts, and closing underperforming segments of the business.
- "Roll-up" strategies are common. A fund first buys a well-run anchor business with top-notch management, systems, and technology, and likely pays a premium for it. Then they purchase additional businesses in the same industry, perhaps dozens, that are poorly run and cheaper, placing them under the anchor. After stabilizing, they have a very large, well-run operation ready to go public.
- Other buyout funds target public companies and take them private. They may have seen their stock price crash or fallen out of favor with investors, but still have a compelling business. After the business is purchased, its shares are delisted from the stock exchanges. Public companies have heavy regulatory burdens—such as Sarbanes-Oxley—along with high public scrutiny, forced short-term focus because of quarterly reporting requirements, and sometimes a dysfunctional board of directors. Going private can eliminate these issues, giving the company time to sort out its operations and potentially go public again later. It can be easier to find and negotiate with a target company, because the information is public, and the price is already set by the stock market.

Growth funds are very similar, but typically buy minority stakes in operating business. They usually don't use debt leverage. A minority stake means the sponsor influences rather than controls the company. Growth funds typically focus on earlier-stage businesses in the growth phase with solid operations and high growth potential.

Secondaries funds buy private equity stakes from existing LPs. Often, the selling fund or LP needs liquidity or wants to rebalance their portfolio. For buyers, it is an opportunity to acquire PE stakes with a shorter duration and reduced risk, as the earliest stages of PE tend to be the riskiest.

Distressed funds buy companies often out of bankruptcy, fix them, and later go public. Often, the major source of distress is debt, which is solved through the purchase.

> **Private equity offers investors a proven path to higher returns.**

Fund-of-funds focus on selecting the best private equity managers and monitoring their performance. Since manager selection is the most important part of PE investing, they can add significant value. They often maintain relationships with the top managers and usually offer smaller investment entry points. The downside is the extra layer of fees.

PE firms often charge "2/20"—that is, 2 percent of the value of the fund every year and 20 percent of the profits when a deal is exited. In more recent years, fees have been dropping toward "1/10." Many PE funds also have a "hurdle rate" provision, meaning they only charge their profits fee for amounts exceeding the hurdle rate (for example, investors must first earn an 8 percent annual return on their capital, and the sponsor gets 20 percent of the profits above that).

Caution

There is a reason that private equity is Level 3 on the Alts Continuum. It is very challenging for a private investor to get access to and do the necessary due diligence on the hundreds of potential opportunities. On this topic, David Swensen warned:

> In the absence of truly superior fund selection skills (or extraordinary luck) investors should stay far, far away from private equity investments.[43]

David also mentioned staying away from larger funds, above $1 billion, citing how management incentives change as successful funds grow:

> As fund size increases, fee income becomes an increasingly significant profit center. As fee income grows, general partner behavior changes, focusing on protecting the firm's franchise and maintaining the annuity like character of the stream of fees. Larger buyout funds pursue less risky deals, employing lower levels of leverage. The big partnerships devote more time to cultivating and nourishing limited partner relationships, the source of the funds (and fees). Less time remains for investment activity. Returns suffer.
>
> For the 20 years ending June 30th, 2003, Cambridge Associates data show that buyout funds with more than $1 billion of committed capital produce returns of 6.0% per year. In contrast funds under $1 billion returned 17.8% per year, a dramatically superior result.[44]

When you are ready to invest in private equity, I would recommend starting with a fund-of-funds investment. It will cost you slightly lower returns due to the added layer of fees but allow you diversification into multiple PE deals with a smaller check size, and likely keep you from making a very poor sponsor choice, all the while teaching you the ropes of private equity.

Private equity offers investors a proven path to higher returns, portfolio diversification, and direct ownership in high-growth businesses. By investing in private companies, you gain access to opportunities that are often out of reach for the average investor, with the potential for substantial long-term wealth creation.

To explore our latest thoughts on private equity opportunities, visit investlikeabillionaire.org/book.

Next, we'll take this concept a step further with venture capital—a high-risk, high-reward asset class focused on companies with explosive growth potential.

CHAPTER 9

VENTURE CAPITAL

*"Given a 10% chance of a 100 times payoff,
you should take that bet every time."*
— **Jeff Bezos**

I always had a bit of an entrepreneurial itch. In 1995, I wrote a business plan, one of the worst in the history of mankind, raised $100,000 from my mom, quit my well-paying job, hired my sister-in-law, and started my Internet business in my attic. After multiple brushes with imminent (business) death, we pivoted successfully and began growing like crazy.

Then, out of the blue, I got a call from a venture capital firm.

We ended up raising $44 million in venture capital in three rounds and found ourselves right in the middle of the dot-com craze. My VC-packed board of directors put us on a fast-growth track, turning my marginally profitable company into a hypergrowth cash-burning machine fueled by their capital. In 1999, we were the fastest-growing business in the Midwest, our revenues doubling every three to four months. We hired like mad, reaching 280 employees. In 2000, I won the Ernst & Young Entrepreneur of the Year award. We hired an investment banker to sponsor our IPO later that year.

Then, a competitor who had gone public a few years earlier reported poor earnings, just as the dot-com bubble was popping. Their stock was crushed. I was euphoric.

But at our next board meeting, I found the VCs suddenly disinterested in the business and talking about ways to wind it down!

The lights were switched on for me. When our competitor crashed, our comparative value crashed too. It didn't matter that our revenues were exploding. The window for our IPO—the VCs' planned exit—had closed. And still burning cash like mad, we would have to raise more funds. But the market was closed for that too. We ended up liquidating the business.

It was a stark lesson in the fickleness of the stock market. It was a devastating loss, but it turned out to be a gold mine of experience for me.

HOW VENTURE CAPITAL WORKS

One of my first investors was a somewhat famous venture capital investor. He said their formula was simple: Invest in companies that could potentially generate a 100x return on exit. They needed just one in eighteen to work, and the other seventeen were immaterial. It was putting eighteen chips on the roulette table and betting that one would hit.

Venture capital is a special class of private equity. VCs buy stakes in high-growth startups, grow them, and groom them for IPO.

VC funds typically focus on a handful of specialty areas, like healthcare, or fintech. They love technology primarily because it can scale so well. VC firms are usually classified by their preferred investment stage.

Angel funds invest very, very early, when the company is little more than an idea. They are smaller and put in a few hundred thousand. Most startups at this stage fail, and these funds are extremely risky.

Years ago, after my dot-com business implosion, I joined an angel fund. Sixty guys, mostly successful doctors and lawyers, each put in $50,000. We took investor pitches and voted on whether or not to invest.

We invested in two dozen deals and watched all of them fizzle out over the next few years. I learned that being smart in one area makes people think they are smart in every area! And a democracy cannot build a good angel portfolio.

Seed capital funds are very early, typically providing funding for product prototypes or development. Funds are usually small, and the funds typically invest in the $500,000 to $2 million range.

Growth stage funds invest when a company has a successful "proof of concept" in the market and some revenues. Capital is used to scale growth. As the company grows, there are multiple funding rounds, each larger than the last, called Series A, B, and C. Check sizes might be $5 million to $50 million.

Late stage (expansion) funds invest when the company is on the verge of IPO. Funds might be used to strengthen the balance sheet as they make their final push for the public markets. They are larger rounds and considered less risky since the company has visibility of their exit.

Caution

Many wealthy people make investments into a family or friend's business idea and call it "venture capital." Please know you are virtually assured of 100 percent loss, and even worse, often destroy the relationships as well. This is technically called *angel investing*, and certainly not the kind of professional venture capital fund investing we are covering here.

Performance

Again, with the usual caveats regarding data biases and averages, let's look at how VCs performed in crashes and booms.

In the dot-com crash, not surprisingly VCs were crushed, and continued to underperform even in the subsequent boom. But venture capital eventually recovered and performed very well in the two other crashes and also in their subsequent booms.

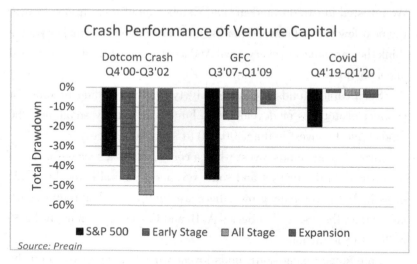

Figure 45: Crash Performance of Venture Capital

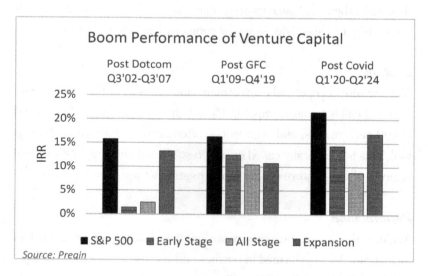

Figure 46: Boom Performance of Venture Capital

Venture capital's risk/return metrics below show much lower risk than the public markets, and lower returns as well. Don't be overly dissuaded by the poor return numbers in these charts. This is due to the timing of my data, which starts at the dot-com crash. If we eliminate the dot-com and post-dot-com periods, returns are a solid 7.8–10.3 percent IRR. This is a poignant reminder that in analyzing financial data, the time period selected will wildly affect your results; and indexes and averages can be materially misleading.

Proceed with Care

Venture capital is very unique in that a handful of top-tier firms dominate the space. Because of their reputation, contacts, and expertise, the best prospects seek them out. These firms do not accept new capital and even ration capital from existing investors. This leaves you with the prospect that firms that do accept your capital represent less attractive opportunities. David Swensen commented, "Unfortunately for investors, the promise of venture capital exceeds the reality."[45] Swensen's long-standing relationships with top-tier firms gave him access to their funds. But he

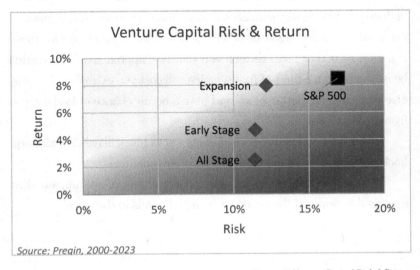

Figure 47: Venture Capital Risk & Return

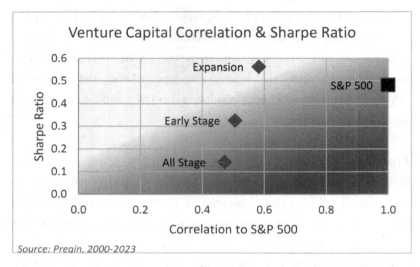

Figure 48: Venture Capital S&P 500 Correlation and Sharpe Ratio

mused that if he were starting out fresh, he might avoid venture capital altogether.[46]

VC fund investing is not for the novice. As with all alts, there is a very high dispersion among managers, making manager selection paramount; extraordinary effort must be taken—and best in conjunction with those experienced in doing so. I recommend your first approach to VC investing be made through a fund-of-funds, which will cost you extra fees, but may give you access to better funds and have a better chance of keeping you from losses.

If you want to explore your options, go to investlikeabillionaire.org/book to see our latest thoughts and recommendations.

Next up are hedge funds, those playgrounds of the ultrawealthy managed by some of the smartest financial minds in the world.

CHAPTER 10

HEDGE FUNDS

> *"A hedge fund is a compensation scheme masquerading as an asset class."*
> **- Warren Buffet**

Hedge funds exist in the popular mind as shadowy enterprises run by "type A" tycoons out to dominate the financial world, like Gordon Gecko from the 1987 movie *Wall Street*. But hedge funds play an important role in the portfolio of the ultrawealthy. You'll see why.

WHAT IS A HEDGE FUND?

Hedge funds differ from all other private alts in that they invest primarily in publicly traded securities, similar to exchange-traded funds (ETFs) or mutual funds. However, unlike those traditional vehicles, hedge funds are (mostly) *unregulated*—so they can invest in complex derivatives, swaps and options, commodities, currencies, and futures. They can also *short* markets, bets that make money when values drop. They often employ various hedging strategies to limit exposure to the movement of stock markets, interest rates, or currencies. Here are some of the strategies they employ:

Convertible arbitrage funds seek to exploit the mispricing between convertible securities and the corresponding stock, usually buying the convertible and shorting the stock.

Emerging markets hedge funds invest in any number of strategies. *Emerging markets* refer to stocks in underdeveloped countries. Often these stocks trade at deep discounts to developed markets, outperform in good times, and underperform in bad times.

Equity neutral hedge funds attempt to invest so that they profit whether the general market goes up or down, typically by balancing long and short positions, or otherwise hedging out exposure to the general stock market.

Absolute return funds are similar to equity neutral funds but strive to take even less exposure to the direction of the stock market, aiming for a certain return in all markets.

Event-driven funds invest in mispricing related to corporate or market events—things like mergers, acquisitions, bankruptcies, spin-offs, splits, restructurings, etc.

Distressed funds invest in companies in distressed situations that tend to trade at a discount to intrinsic value.

Fixed income arbitrage funds attempt to make money on mispricing in the bond markets. They often try to hedge out exposure to interest rates and stock markets.

Global macro funds typically forecast global macroeconomic and/or political trends, anticipating the movements of equities, bonds, currencies, etc.

Relative value (long / short) funds take long positions in stocks they consider undervalued and short positions in stocks they consider overvalued. They are betting on the relative performance of one stock over another while being neutral to the overall market.

Managed futures funds invest in the futures markets, often in commodities like oil, lumber, or wheat.

This is only the briefest overview of hedge fund strategies, but for your purposes in seeking to invest like a billionaire, the thumbnail summaries provide the information you need to move forward.

There are thousands of hedge funds with the cleverest strategies imaginable. They employ some of the most brilliant minds in the financial world. For a finance nerd like me, it's hard not to be impressed. But recall the debacle of hedge fund LTCM (chapter 4) and its two Nobel Prize-winners—brilliance doesn't always get results.

The Problem with Hedge Funds

As you can tell by the strategies employed, hedge funds usually attempt various forms of hedging to limit risks. That costs money, and if those risks never materialize, it is a drag on performance. Thus, when the stock market is strong, hedge funds typically underperform. You can see both the limited risk and the performance drag in the charts below. Surprisingly, in the dot-com crash, hedge funds went up. And in the other two crashes, hedge funds showed fewer losses than the stock market. And in our three boom periods, hedge funds underperformed the markets.

Hedge funds also charge fees—typically a management fee in the range of 1–2 percent of assets under management (AUM) and a performance fee of 15–20 percent of profits. Those fees are also a drag on net performance—the manager must be very good or very lucky to beat the markets by that much. Recall *Figure 18: Public and Private Manager Dispersion* (p. 71)—the data shows that it is nearly impossible to consistently beat the public markets. And the data here proves it: Even the genius professionals running hedge funds often cannot generate enough excess returns to cover the fees they charge.

What Makes Hedge Funds Attractive

Given the performance lag and fees, what exactly is the appeal of hedge funds to the ultrawealthy? Here is the basic idea: to earn *equity-like returns*

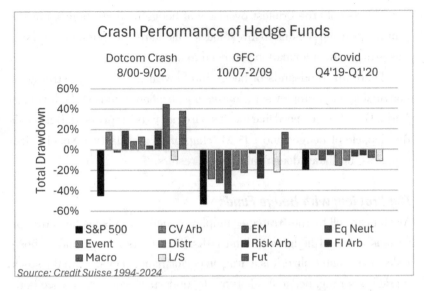

Fig 49: Crash Performance of Hedge Funds.png

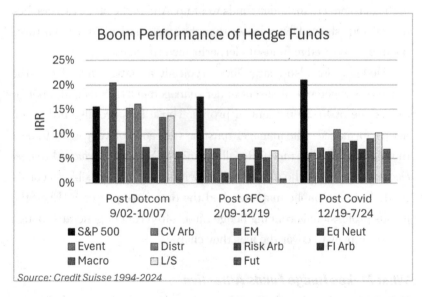

Figure 50: Boom Performance of Hedge Funds

with *bond-like risk*. The ultrawealthy are not trying to match or beat the markets but to earn decent returns with limited risk and low correlations. Many use hedge funds as a "bond substitute." Hedge funds underperform the markets but can offer better risk-adjusted returns and, sometimes, extraordinarily low correlations.

The results validate their reasoning. Let's look at the fifteen years prior to the Great Financial Crisis. Throughout the Internet boom of the 1990s, hedge funds lagged. But in the subsequent bust, the hedge funds avoided the worst of the losses.

Similarly, in the Great Financial Crisis of 2007–2008, hedge funds were able to minimize losses. By doing so in these two crashes, hedge fund investors far outperformed index investors in this period, gaining 250 percent compared to 50 percent. One of the main lessons of this book is that *volatility destroys compounding*—and thus *minimizing losses is more important than maximizing gains*. The above chart is a graphic picture of this principle. It didn't matter that hedge funds lagged in the booms; by avoiding the worst drawdowns, they handily beat the market overall.

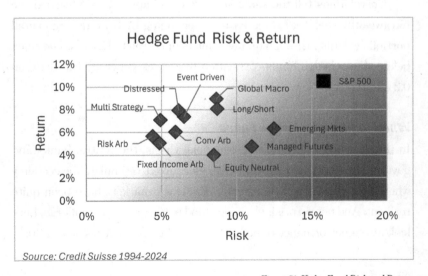

Figure 51: Hedge Fund Risk and Return

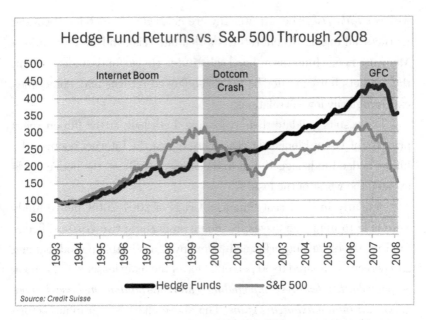

Figure 52: Hedge Fund Returns vs. S&P 500 Through 2008

Correlations tell the same story. From chapter 4, you learned the ultrawealthy seek to: (a) increase compounding by (b) reducing overall portfolio volatility through (c) investing in uncorrelated assets. The chart below shows hedge funds correlation to a stock generally run between 0.2 and 0.7—very low.

When to Invest in Hedge Funds

In the aftermath of the Great Financial Crisis, the central banks and governments have taken more active measures to stimulate the economy when challenges arise. As a result, the stock markets have been quite resilient. And not surprisingly, hedge fund performance has suffered. Let's look at the performance of hedge funds in the fifteen years since 2009.

HEDGE FUNDS   151

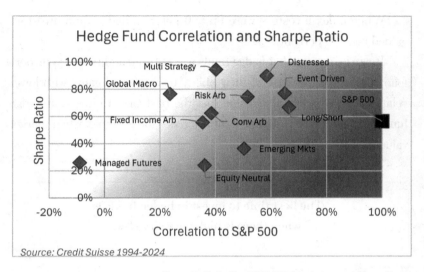

Figure 53: Hedge Fund S&P 500 Correlations and Sharpe Ratios

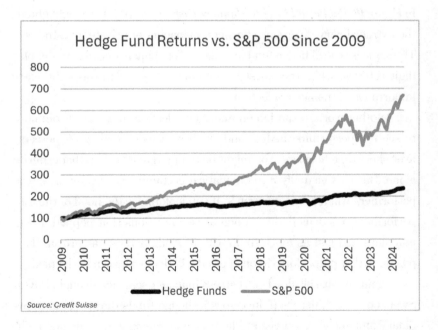

Figure 54: Hedge Fund Returns vs. S&P 500 Since 2009

While index investors were up 580 percent, hedge fund investors gained just 140 percent.

It can be argued that hedge funds are a strong addition to your portfolio at any time because of their ability to earn solid gains with lower volatility. But I would also argue that the best time to invest in hedge funds is when there is higher volatility risk—for example, when market valuations are high.

> The best time to invest in hedge funds is when there is high volatility risk.

Hedge Fund Selection

In *Figure 18: Public and Private Manager Dispersion* (p. 71), we highlighted the extraordinary divergence between managers of private investments. The same is true of hedge fund managers. Top managers can earn double-digit returns, while the worst lose money. This underscores the vast importance of manager selection.

Another word of caution on manager selection: It is not uncommon to see top-performing hedge funds with returns exceeding 50 percent over short time horizons. You might be tempted to invest on that criteria alone. But it is virtually a mathematical certainty that yesterday's top performers will not be tomorrow's. If you look under the hood of the top performers, it's usually due to one or two positions that popped. Luck may have had just as much to do with it. And analysis has proven that positions that outperform in one period will underperform in the next.

Again, as with all alts, I can't stress manager selection enough. David Swensen said, "Successful investors in hedge funds devote an extraordinary amount of resources to identifying engaging and managing high

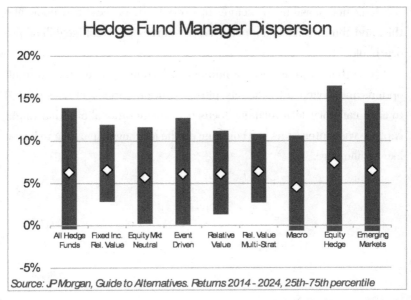

Figure 55: Hedge Fund Manager Dispersion

quality managers. Casual approaches to hedge fund selection lead to almost certain disappointment... Hedge fund investing belongs in the domain of sophisticated investors who commit significant resources to the manager evaluation process."[47]

There is another hedge fund strategy worth considering: fund-of-funds (FOF). These are hedge funds that invest in other hedge funds. They do due diligence as well as allocate and manage the holdings. Many fund-of-funds are much smaller than the funds they invest in, and their managers are more accessible. In addition, hedge funds can have eight-figure minimums, while fund-of-funds are usually much lower. Many avoid fund-of-funds because of the additional layer of fees. But for someone wanting to make a sophisticated initial approach to hedge funds or allocate smaller amounts, they could be a smart choice.

It is not possible to include up-to-date resources in a book like this, and thus we have compiled free resources at investlikeabillionaire.org/book.

Now that we've covered a number of frequently chosen private alt options and looked at the details, pluses, cautions, and strategies related to each category, let's turn our focus to some additional alts that might capture your interest as you continue on the journey of learning to invest like a billionaire.

CHAPTER 11

OIL & GAS, GOLD, CRYPTO, AND MORE

"My formula for success is rise early, work late, and strike oil."
- J. P. Getty

It's time to cover a few other popular alternatives. First, is one that for a century has minted thousands of millionaires and billionaires—oil and gas.

OIL AND GAS

Oil and gas investment is a very unique space:
- Very high cash flows
- Strong tax incentives
- High discounts due to unpopularity
- High volatility of underlying commodities
- Plethora of marginal opportunities aimed at retail investors

Oil and gas is the largest subcategory of natural resources investment. Recall *Figure 25: Private Alts Risk and Return* (p. 90) and *Figure 26: Private Alts S&P 500 Correlation and Sharpe Ratio* (p. 90). This class has one of the best risk-adjusted return profiles and lowest correlation to stocks.

Are Fossil Fuels Obsolete?

There is a popular narrative that the world no longer needs fossil fuels. To quote the International Energy Agency (IEA), a forum organized under twenty-nine nations of the OECD, "As clean energy expands and fossil fuel demand declines in the NZE Scenario, *there is no need for investment in new coal, oil and natural gas*" (emphasis added). They predict fossil fuel demand to drop by more than 25 percent by 2030 and 80 percent by 2050.[48] That is completely unrealistic. Fossil fuels comprised 81 percent of fuel usage in 2023, after fifty years of pushing toward renewables. And oil is used for 91 percent of global transportation. Oil's high energy density makes it extremely difficult to replace.

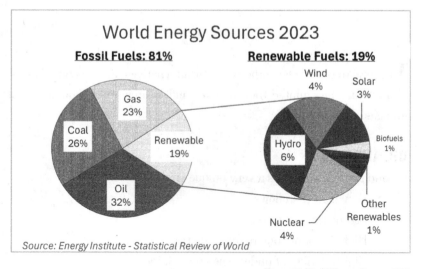

Figure 56: World Energy Sources 2023

However unlikely, this narrative has gained popularity and caused oil and gas exploration and development funding globally to drop by half between 2015 and 2024. Investment capital has been driven away from the sector, making oil and gas investments historically inexpensive, and setting the stage for future energy shortages.

Ways to Invest

When done properly, oil and gas investment can be one of your best-performing assets. Here are the main ways you can invest:

1. **Mineral Rights / Royalty Interests.** Land has mineral rights, which can be sold separately. When an oil producer wants to develop the land, they must sign a lease with the mineral rights holder, specifying the royalties to be paid on production, typically 15–25 percent of the gross production value.

    Mineral rights owners typically do not pay taxes on the land and do not share any costs related to development or production.

    The advantages are clear, but there are serious disadvantages. You might hold the rights for decades without any producer taking interest.

2. **Working Interests.** You may also invest in working interests. This means you share in a percentage of the costs as well as the profits. You typically invest with the operator, who makes all operational decisions.

    The risks and rewards are high. Exploration and development costs are high, cost overruns are common, as are uneconomical wells.

3. **Non-Operated Working Interests.** This is a similar to above, except the operator is a third party. The investor is not responsible for operations but is consulted on major expenditures. The main advantage is that typically the operators in these arrangements are larger "majors" with top staff, technology, and experience.

4. **Midstream and Downstream Investments.** Production-related projects are termed *upstream*. *Midstream* projects are pipelines and depots that deliver and store oil and gas, and *downstream* projects are refiners, processors, and terminals.

Investment Stages

Oil and gas wells have mathematically calculated *reserves*, detailing the size and extent of hydrocarbons present. Reserves have three mathematical and legal categories:

1. **Proven** reserves have a 90 percent probability of successful extraction,
2. **Probable** reserves have a 50 percent probability, and
3. **Possible** reserves have at least a 10 percent probability.

As geologists drill test holes and examine the results, the size of the reserves increases, and the quality of the reserves improves, for example from *probable* to *proven*.

This leads to three development stages with decreasing levels of risk:

1. **Exploration** projects drill test wells to find oil and gas reserves—obviously quite risky—though modern geologists have extraordinary technologies available to increase the likelihood of positive outcomes.

    Few investments are offered at this stage due to the extraordinary risks.

2. **Development** projects, called PUD (proven, undeveloped), drill production wells into proven reserves. If sufficient minerals are encountered, the wells are *completed*, meaning the pumping and extraction infrastructure is purchased and placed into operation.

Completion costs as much as 80 percent of development costs, so failed wells are not as costly as completed wells.

Many investments are offered at this stage, but significant risks remain—some geologic risk, as well as potentially significant engineering risks.

3. **Producing** projects, called PDP (proven, developed, producing), purchase completed, producing wells, eliminating most geologic risks.

All oil and gas production suffers from depletion—production falls off over time. Production decline curves vary widely by location, but the greatest production declines are at the beginning.

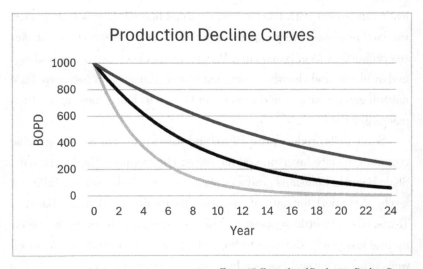

Figure 57: Examples of Production Decline Curves

Thus, even producing investments come with the significant risk of value decreasing over time. Most sponsors who focus on producing investments therefore continually invest in some development programs in order to keep steady cash flows and to maintain the value of the assets for future sale.

Oil vs. Natural Gas

Oil is an extremely important commodity due to its extraordinarily high energy density. Practically, this has made oil very difficult to replace by renewable technologies, and oil remains the power behind 91 percent of global transportation—autos, trucks, airplanes, trains, and ships. There is little other way to get as much energy in as small a package, and that matters if you must take your energy with you.

Natural gas is very different. Because it is in a gaseous state, it takes about 6,000 cubic feet of natural gas to equal the same amount of energy as a single barrel (42 gallons) of oil. This makes gas uneconomical to transport with trucks, rail, or ships like oil. Gas is transported via fixed pipelines—very expensive and difficult to construct. *This makes gas primarily a local commodity*. Wherever pipelines exist, gas is cheap and available, and elsewhere, very expensive. Europe and Asia have little natural gas resources, and prices can be two to four times higher than places like the US.

Some wells produce primarily oil and others primarily gas. Geographic regions typically favor one or the other. For example, the Haynesville Shale Basin in Louisiana produces primarily gas. Each basin has different levels of support for natural gas. Another locale, the Permian Basin in Texas, has very little support, and oil producers are forced to flare their natural gas production due to the lack of pipelines for offtake. Most oil wells produce natural gas as a byproduct of oil production.

Natural gas has become the primary power source for electricity production, due to the increasing unpopularity of coal. It also has low carbon output (50–60 percent less than coal) and is inexpensive. Natural gas power turbines can be quickly deployed and quickly brought online and taken offline to meet variable power demands.

Liquefied natural gas (LNG) is natural gas that has been compressed and cooled to -260° F. LNG accounts for roughly 10 percent of global natural gas consumption but is growing rapidly. LNG is in high demand in places like Europe and Asia. However, its extremely cold temperatures make it very difficult to produce, transport, and handle. It requires dedicated production facilities, purpose-built ships, and onload-offload terminals.

Vertical vs. Horizontal Drilling
Historically drilling was vertical: A spot was chosen, and a vertical well was drilled straight down. In the 2000s, horizontal drilling became predominant. From a single location, many holes can be drilled for miles in any direction. A single well can service a much larger area. Horizontal wells are ideal for shale geologies because they are layered. Vertical wells can only reach reservoirs directly beneath them, while horizontal wells can reach multiple reservoirs. Horizontal wells are much more expensive and much more complex to drill and operate, but they drain a far larger area, and, despite their expense, are more cost-effective. Small operators rarely have the expertise to use horizontal drilling.

Commodity Pricing
One of the greatest risks in oil and gas investment, as with all natural resource investing, is commodity pricing. Oil prices are notoriously volatile, and natural gas even more so due to its hyper-local availability and its weather-driven demand.

As noted above, in the 2000s, horizontal drilling revolutionized oil and gas production in the US, and the next fifteen years saw exponential growth, making the US the number one oil producer in the world and upsetting the global order. Saudi Arabia decided to exert its dominance, ramping up production to crush oil prices, and in 2016, oil fell to $26 per barrel, below the production costs of many US producers.

To maintain debt payments, producers were forced to ramp up production, driving prices down even further. Hundreds of producers went bankrupt. Prices crashed again in 2020, this time going negative—producers paid refiners to take their oil. Today most operators are very cautious and highly disciplined, using minimal debt and employing hedging strategies to protect against price crashes.

> **Make sure your sponsors are lightly levered or hedged to weather price storms.**

Make sure that your sponsors are lightly levered or hedged to weather any price storms.

Taxes

Oil and gas investing has the most beneficial tax treatment of any sector. Here are a few of the major benefits:

- **Depletion allowance.** Investors owe taxes on 85 percent of gross income, a 15 percent automatic discount.
- **Tangible drilling costs**, the "hard" costs of drilling, are 100 percent tax-deductible, depreciated over seven years.
- **Intangible drilling costs**, the "soft" costs of drilling, which account for 60–80 percent of drilling costs, are 100 percent tax-deductible the year they are incurred.
- **Active income.** Working interests (but not royalty interests) are considered active, and thus any losses can be deducted from active income like wages. This makes oil and gas stand alone in the world of investments, and, for high earners, makes oil and gas investing compelling.

Selecting Investments

Oil and gas seems to be an area filled with marginal operators targeting individual investors with exaggerated claims.

One sponsor was selling interests in a single vertical well, at a 10x markup from cost. Obviously, putting a large amount of capital in a single drill opportunity is very risky. And at a 10x markup, even a successful well could never yield good returns.

Pay special attention to:

- **Sponsors leading with large year-one tax benefits**, which mean they are primarily drilling.
- **Drilling-only plays**, which, in addition to the expected commodity pricing risks, also carry geological risks, engineering risks, and operator skill risks.
- **Vertical wells**, which are risker and less economical than horizontal wells.
- **Smaller operators**, who probably lack the top geologists and engineers generally required for success.

Swensen commented, "It was difficult to find well-designed oil-and-gas partnerships led by attractive managers. Many of the partnerships appeared to be in the hands of agents, who were compensated primarily on the basis of arranging deals. A number of operators seemed to get rich even if their clients did not. Furthermore, assessing the skills of the general partners in these funds was often difficult."[49]

He therefore focused on deals that focused on acquiring existing oil fields and enhancing their operations. "In contrast to the high-risk world of exploration, assessing performance and responsibility in the reserve acquisitions arena was somewhat easier. Furthermore, the long-term assets provided relatively predictable income." Swensen liked natural resources for their sensitivity to commodity prices, which provided an important hedge against inflation.[50]

Great oil and gas investments are very difficult to source. This is because most of the best opportunities have been family-owned for decades, and they don't need outside capital. However, they can be found. Check out our resources at investlikeabillionaire.org/book.

OTHER NATURAL RESOURCES

Oil and gas is one example of natural resources investing, but there are other subcategories like timber, farmland, and mining. These areas don't attract as much capital as energy but can have the advantage of high returns and being highly uncorrelated.

INFRASTRUCTURE

Infrastructure is another hidden gem that is typically underrepresented in most portfolios. Look again at *Figure 25: Private Alts Risk and Return* (p. 90) and at *Figure 26: Private Alts S&P 500 Correlation and Sharpe Ratio* (p. 90). Infrastructure has perhaps the most compelling risk-adjusted returns and low correlations of any alts class.

Infrastructure investments include energy (pipelines, storage, refining, and terminals), utility projects (power plants and water treatment facilities), transportation projects (toll roads, airports, terminals, and ports), and social projects (schools, hospitals, courts, and correction facilities). Most infrastructure deals are in energy (63 percent) followed by transportation (12 percent) and utilities (10 percent).[51]

Great infrastructure investments are also very difficult to source. Again, check out our current ideas at investlikeabillionaire.org/book.

MYTHS AND REALITY

If you were to ask a random person on the street, "What is an alternative investment?" the most common answers behind "I don't know" would be "gold" and "crypto." Most of the ultrawealthy, however, typically invest less than 1 percent in these asset classes.

That said, because of the interest in these assets from individual investors, I will give my thoughts on them.

GOLD AND SILVER

Gold and silver have been used as money since the dawn of history. These metals have some wonderful natural properties, as well as scarcity, that made them suitable for currency. They are also difficult to transport and store. Paper currencies gained popularity in the late 1800s but maintained convertibility to the metals. In the early 1900s, central banks emerged to manage national currencies, and all were on the gold standard: The central banks were required to limit the amount of currency in circulation to the amount of gold in their vaults.

Most countries abandoned the gold standard during the 1930s in response to the Great Depression. A vicious cycle had emerged, as people lost jobs, companies folded, and more people lost jobs. There was a need for the government to spend to create artificial demand and break the cycle. On the gold standard, governments and central banks could not do so. As an aside, this is why the US confiscated gold in 1933—to fill their vaults with gold to create more currency to spend.

In the 1930s, one by one, nations exited the gold standard, and as soon as they did so, their national economies began to recover. The US went off the gold standard in March 1933 (the US retained gold convertibility until 1971), which marked the bottom of the Great Depression and the beginning of the economic recovery in the US.[52]

The 1930s demonstrate why the gold standard cannot work, and I don't know of any professional economists who endorse the idea. Unless a currency scales with GDP growth, it will force a nation into a toxic deflation.

Gold and silver retain their allure as investments. I personally love them. They are wonderful to look at! However, as investments, they have a poor track record. Gold has a reputation as an inflation-beater, but except for the 1970s—when gold shot up as the dollar lost convertibility—gold beat inflation in only one decade out of five and even lost value in two of them, as figure 58 illustrates.

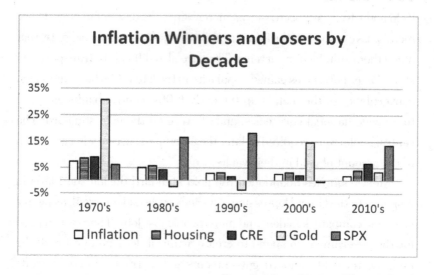

Figure 58: Inflation Winners and Losers by Decade

Gold and silver have a negative yield (they cost money to store), little utility, and are difficult to transport and store. Unless you believe we are headed back to the dark ages via nuclear war, EMP, or solar flare (I don't), I find little reason to own much of either metal.

CRYPTOCURRENCY

Cryptocurrency (like gold) has captured the imagination of a generation. As a computer scientist and a finance professional, I find it fascinating.

Cryptocurrency is based on blockchain technology. Imagine transaction data stored in a data block, and when the block is filled, a new block is created and they are linked together, or "chained." Now imagine every transaction is recorded in these data blocks, starting with initial deposits, like this:

Block	Transaction
1	Bob is awarded 100 Bitcoin
	Fred is awarded 100 Bitcoin
2	Bob transfers 100 Bitcoin to Jim
3	Jim transfers 1 Bitcoin to Frank

If you start at block one and add up every transaction, you can calculate precisely everyone's balance. It's easy to see how much Bitcoin everyone has. Bob has zero, Fred has 100, Jim has 99, and Frank has 1.

Now imagine every transaction is public data, and thousands of computers are continuously updating this same blockchain. It's easy to ask 100 computers how much Bitcoin Bob has, and they will all answer zero. Now let's say Bob is a computer nerd and changes his blockchain to incorrectly show that he has 100 Bitcoin. It's easy to tell he's lying, because the other 99 computers disagree.

Now imagine that instead of people's names, digital wallet IDs are stored. And every wallet ID has a secret key known only to its owner that allows them alone to transact on that wallet ID. How they do all that is fascinating, but I will resist the urge to geek out on the technology. There you have the basics of cryptocurrency.

All cryptocurrencies promise:
- A store of value beyond government reach
- Frictionless cross-border payments
- Transaction privacy

These attributes make cryptocurrency appealing to citizens of nations suffering from hyperinflation or where the governments have implemented capital controls or wealth confiscation. But cryptocurrency's strongest value proposition is to facilitate illicit activities. There is only one cryptocurrency I know of that has potential as an investment.

Cryptocurrencies have a long way to go to become mainstream currencies for several reasons:

- Governments will protect their rights of seigniorage—the manufacturing of money—for its enormous benefits to the issuer.
- Authorities will always want to control currency movements to track illicit trade.
- By controlling the gateways where currencies are converted to and from cryptocurrencies, governments can effectively limit cryptocurrency adoption.

There are thousands of cryptocurrencies, but I pay attention to only three.

Bitcoin

Bitcoin is the first and oldest cryptocurrency. Here are some quick facts:

- Only 21 million Bitcoin will ever exist.[53] This has made Bitcoin attractive as a speculative asset. It has replaced gold as the alternative currency of choice for many "hard money" enthusiasts, because, like gold, it cannot be debased by overproduction. But unlike gold, it is easy to transport, can easily support very large positions, and does not have a negative yield because it is free to store.
- Only seven transactions per second can be recorded in the global Bitcoin blockchain.[54] This is a structural limitation that cannot be changed, making it incapable of becoming a global payment system (the Visa system can handle 65,000 transactions per second).
- Bitcoin consumes enormous electrical power. This is due to its archaic "proof-of-work" methodology whereby millions of

computers compete to solve a complex math problem requiring trillions of calculations, to be awarded the bounty in creating a new block. Modern systems have upgraded to a "proof-of-stake" concept.
- Bitcoin, like all cryptocurrencies, is not anonymous, but *pseudonymous*. Every transaction is public knowledge, as is every wallet ID. You can track every transaction ever done by everyone—but you cannot tell who a wallet ID belongs to. But when cryptocurrency is converted to real currency, the authorities can tie wallets to individuals.

Bitcoin is unique among cryptocurrencies in that it has significant adoption, little counterparty or operator risk, and the number of Bitcoin is capped. As long as there is any net demand for Bitcoin, its value must rise, because supply cannot. I believe Bitcoin will continue to attract some demand and thus I believe it will rise in value over time. And like all cryptocurrencies, it has appeal to those who desire privacy and have concern over government overreach. I like Bitcoin as something of a "speculative insurance policy," but I don't believe it deserves a place as a core holding in your portfolio.

Ether

Ether is the cryptocurrency built into Ethereum. Ethereum was conceived as a global blockchain infrastructure. If you want to build a custom blockchain application or service, you will probably build it on Ethereum—otherwise you must convince thousands of computer operators to run your code 24/7. Ethereum provides a ready-made infrastructure. There are thousands of blockchain applications built on top of Ethereum, as well as thousands of other cryptocurrencies.

Unlike Bitcoin, Ethereum is actively developed. It is now on a proof-of-stake model, so it doesn't require lots of power. Ethereum is still limited to about twelve transactions per second, not enough to power a global payment system, but they will likely continue to improve it.

Because of Ethereum's position as essential infrastructure for all blockchain applications, it is interesting as a technology, but I find nothing compelling as an investment.

Tether

Tether is a "stablecoin"—it is designed to track the value of the US dollar, making it in essence a "digital dollar." Dealers wire funds to Tether Holdings, its operator, who issues new coins. They use the money to buy US Treasury securities and claim that all Tether is backed by deposits. Its $1 price is maintained through arbitrageurs, who can buy Tether at $0.99 if it drops there and redeem in for $1.

Tether has gained popularity as the ultimate crypto dollar. It is appealing because it is tied to the US dollar. According to the *Wall Street Journal*, Tether is the top choice for those in nations suffering from hyperinflation. But it is also the preferred choice for drug traffickers, money launderers, weapons dealers, and terrorist groups, and the means by which sanctioned nations bypass sanctions.[55] Unlike Bitcoin, Tether is centrally operated out of the British Virgin Islands by a secretive group of owners, and its value is maintained by its investment portfolio, which, like any counterparty, is subject to fraud or mismanagement.

> **It is wise to approach these investments with an extra note of care and caution.**

Tether is interesting as an international monetary phenomenon but is very unattractive as an investment, having significant risks and no associated returns.

A WORD OF CAUTION

When it comes to potential investments like those outlined in this chapter—and which have taken their turns in the public spotlight as trendy or hot possibilities over the years—the same principles that apply to all forms of private alts apply here as well. Even so, it is wise to consider these investments with an extra note of care and caution.

With all of that in mind, let's pivot toward a much more traditional and well-known investment avenue—stocks and bonds—and examine the lessons and insights billionaires can show us about the best ways to invest.

CHAPTER 12

STOCKS AND BONDS

"One of the funny things about the stock market is that every time one person buys, another sells, and both think they are astute."
- William Feather

This book is about the power of private alternatives. But stocks and bonds also play an important role in the portfolios of the ultrawealthy. However, they invest in the stock market very differently than the average investor, and in this chapter, I will give you the billionaire's stock market playbook. We are fortunate that David Swensen shared his playbook, and we will quote from it generously in this chapter.

MARKET TIMING

The first thing is that the ultrawealthy are not market timers. They are not trying to beat the market.

Swensen specifically mentioned data from *Morningstar* that compared time-weighted returns to dollar-weighted returns. Time-weighted returns are what you would typically think of—the performance of the investment over time. Dollar-weighted returns are what returns investors actually made, accounting for the timing of their investments. Data shows that overwhelmingly, investors hurt themselves by buying at the top and selling at the bottom.[56] We talked about these emotional mistakes in chapter 4. Humans are inevitably victims of their emotional wiring. Swensen commented, "The individual has almost no chance of beating the market."[57]

The ultrawealthy invest in the stock market primarily to get access to the world's largest and best companies. Data shows that over the last one hundred years, investing in the stock market has returned roughly 10 percent per year. And in stretches, like the ten years 2015–2024, it's over 13 percent, and the two years 2023–24, 28 percent. That's incredible.

But between 1929 and 1932, you would have lost 65 percent of your capital in the S&P. And if you were in the broader market of smaller stocks, it would have been 90 percent. Swensen called it watching your "dollars turning into dimes!"[58]

The ultrawealthy want exposure to the public markets but without giving them the power to wipe out their portfolio.

Swensen "believed that risk could be more effectively reduced by limiting aggregate exposure to any single asset class, rather than by attempting to time markets. While Swensen and his staff usually had their own informed views of the economy and markets, they believed that those views were usually reflected in market prices. They thus tended to avoid trying to time short-run market fluctuations and would overweight or underweight an asset class only if a persuasive case could be made that market prices were measurably misvalued for understandable reasons."[59]

INDEX INVESTING

Yale was an early adopter of *index investing*, which focuses on purchasing groups of stocks rather than individual shares. The most popular way of doing this today is to buy shares of an ETF (exchange-traded fund). For example, one of the largest is SPY. You can purchase SPY like any other stock. But in doing so, you are buying shares in the 500 largest stocks in the market. When you buy or sell shares, the sponsor purchases or sells shares in all 500 stocks in the S&P 500 Index. SPY is thus called an *index tracking stock* because it tracks the underlying index.

There are thousands of similar ETFs that track other indexes. Mutual funds similarly often track indexes.

Interestingly, Swensen moved away from index investing after a time.

> Although Yale had been an early adopter of indexing in the late 1970s, as the Investments Office staff became increasingly confident in its ability to find superior managers it eliminated the passive portfolio in favor of a small number of active equity managers. These managers shared several characteristics. First, most of Yale's active equity managers emphasized disciplined approaches to investing that could be clearly articulated and differentiated from others. Swensen and Takahashi were convinced that disciplined fundamental-based approaches, when intelligently applied, could generate reliable and superior long-run performance. Not surprisingly, none of Yale's managers tended to emphasize market timing, nor did they use fuzzy or abstrusely intuitive investment approaches. The university's managers tended to be smaller independent organizations that were owned by their investment professionals. Other things being equal, Yale preferred managers willing to co-invest and to be compensated commensurate with their investment performance.[60]

REBALANCING

Over time, your portfolio allocations will drift simply because of the mix of winners and losers. For example, say you allocated 5 percent of your portfolio to SPY, but after a year, it has grown to 8 percent. Smart investors have a *rebalancing strategy*. This means that at various intervals, you buy and sell as needed to return to your target portfolio allocation. In the example, you would sell enough SPY shares to bring your ownership back to 5 percent.

> **Rebalancing ensures you are buying low and selling high.**

Rebalancing ensures you are *buying low* and *selling high*. It is doing the opposite of market timing!

Here's a real-life example: In the summer of 1987, as stock prices rose, Swensen sold stocks as part of his rebalancing process. After the October crash, when the market dropped 20 percent in a single day, Swensen "repurchased many of the same securities as it sought to bring its asset allocation back to the target level."[61] Simply by rebalancing, he ended up selling high and buying low.

There are three main forms of rebalancing:

- **Calendar based.** Rebalance annually, biannually, or quarterly. This is the most common. Some studies indicate you don't want to rebalance more than once per year.
- **Threshold based.** Rebalance whenever the allocations have drifted materially. One popular form of this—5/25 rebalancing—means to rebalance whenever your larger allocation positions have deviated by 5 percent from their target, and your smaller buckets by 2.5 percent.
- **New money.** Another way to rebalance without selling is to allocate new money to lagging buckets.

Choose whatever works for you; the important thing is to be disciplined. You may not want to trim your winners and buy your losers, but that's exactly the point: Discipline means going against your emotional wiring.

With an alts-heavy portfolio, rebalancing will be a lot lumpier with large rebalancing needed infrequently, but the principle remains core to your success.

INDEX OPTIMIZATION STRATEGIES

There are a number of strategies you can use to increase the performance of index investing, many employed by the ultrawealthy.

One strategy is tax-loss harvesting. In any large index, there will always be some losers. The idea is to sell the losers in the tax year and buy them back later. It can be material, between 1–1.5 percent in increased returns. In order to do this, you cannot own an ETF; you must own the individual shares that make up the index. There are brokerages that will do this for accounts as small as $250,000.

Another strategy is optimizing the stocks that are added to and deleted from the index. Every year roughly twenty stocks are added to or deleted from the S&P 500 Index. Changes are made quarterly. This means that on the last day of the quarter, a handful of shares are sold at any price, and on the next day, a handful of other shares are purchased at any price by the tracking stocks. Because the trades are huge, the shares can crash or spike precipitously. By buying and selling these shares at different times, it is possible to slightly outperform the index. Again, there are funds that can do this for you.

BONDS

Swensen invested roughly 5 percent of their portfolio in bonds. Here are some of the unique ways they treated them:

1. They viewed bonds primarily as a source of "nondisruptive liquidity"—providing liquidity without having to try to sell illiquid assets at steep discounts or sell public equities at market bottoms.

2. They held US Treasuries almost exclusively, avoiding both corporate debt and foreign debt, believing neither compensated investors for the increased risk.
3. They also chose to manage their bond portfolio in-house. Swensen believed that the government bond market was so efficient, and the spread between the performance of government bond fund managers so small, that it did not make sense to hire an outside manager.

Treasuries vs. non-treasuries. Let's look at why Swensen preferred US government Treasury bonds. I took a moment to look up a few rates. Never mind the rates themselves, but the differences:

Bond Type	Yield
US 10-Year Treasury	4.25%
Emerging Markets	3.65%
AAA Corporate	4.72%
BBB Corporate	5.32%

I agree with Swensen that the modest increase in rates for non-treasuries does not compensate for the increase in risk. He also correctly points out that treasuries are the most liquid and efficient market in the world, trading almost $1 trillion per day.

Swensen traded bonds in-house, and if you have a large portfolio, that makes sense. For the rest, just choose a low-cost ETF.

Duration. What duration should you purchase? This of course can change dramatically over time, but let's look at a recent snapshot of interest rates anyhow, again paying attention to the relative yields:

Bond Type	Yield
US 90-day T-bill	4.23%
US 12-month T-bill	4.24%

Bond Type	Yield
US 10-Year Note	4.25%
US 20-Year Note	4.68%
US 30-Year Note	4.60%

Longer-term bonds do not have significantly higher yields. Furthermore, there is a downside. Look at the volatility in the value of the bond stemming from a 1 percent change in interest rates:

Change in Value from a 1% Change in Interest Rates with a 4.5% Coupon	
Bond Type	Value Change
US 90-day T-bill	0.25%
US 12-month T-bill	1.0%
US 10-Year Note	7.6%
US 20-Year Note	12.0%
US 30-Year Note	14.6%

The potentially higher yield of longer bonds does not always compensate for the volatility risk. If the purpose of your bond portfolio is, like Swensen, primarily a source of non-disruptive liquidity, and secondarily an uncorrelated investment, you should stick with short-duration treasuries. The only reason I can see to own long-duration bonds is if you want to speculate on interest rates falling and are willing to take the risk that they won't.

For our latest ideas and approaches to stocks and bonds, visit investlikeabillionaire.org/book.

We have wrapped up our deep dive of private alts categories. Next, we turn to becoming a great private alts investor.

PART 3
ALTS HOW-TO GUIDE

Now that you've learned many of the ins and outs of private alts—what they are, how billionaires think about them—it is time to turn the corner toward applying this knowledge in actionable ways as you begin approaching these kinds of investments.

We'll delve into tax advantages, organization and structure, operator selection, PPMs, and more. Buckle up, because this is where the facts and figures you have been absorbing can turn into investments that might just change your finances and your life.

CHAPTER 13

HOW BILLIONAIRES BEAT THE TAX MAN

"The trick is to stop thinking of it as your money"
- IRS auditor

In 2021, independent news outlet ProPublica dropped a bombshell. Through leaked IRS tax records, they found:

- In 2007 and 2011, multibillionaire Jeff Bezos paid zero in federal income taxes.
- In 2018, Elon Musk, the world's second-richest person, paid zero in federal income taxes.
- Michael Bloomberg once, Carl Icahn two times, and George Soros three times in recent years paid zero in federal income taxes.
- The twenty-five richest Americans saw their collective net worth rise by $401 billion from 2014 to 2018 and paid a total of $13.6 billion in federal income taxes, a tax rate of just 3.4 percent.
- Between 2014 and 2018, Warren Buffett paid 0.10 percent in taxes, Jef Bezos 0.98 percent, Michael Bloomberg 1.30 percent, and Elon Musk 3.27 percent.

- To put that in context, the median American household earned about $70,000 annually and paid 14 percent in federal taxes.[62] Perhaps most astonishing of all: *It was all legal.*

Set aside your outrage for a moment and consider that the tax code is a system of incentives and disincentives designed to drive behavior. *These same tax incentives are available to you.*

We will now show you exactly how they legally dodged taxes, and how you can too.

THE VALUE OF DEFERRING TAXES

Most investors don't know what their *marginal tax rate* is. Your marginal tax rate is the rate you pay on every additional dollar of income. Take a minute and calculate yours: Simply search for "income tax brackets" and find your number. Do it again to find your state. Add the numbers to get an estimate of your marginal tax rate. In the US, you will probably find your rate somewhere between 30 percent and 50 percent.

If you started with $100,000 and compounded 10 percent returns tax-deferred for thirty years, it would be worth $1.75 million. If the gains were taxed at a 40 percent marginal rate, it would only be worth $1.1 million.

It takes effort to minimize taxes, but as the ultrawealthy know, it is well worth it.

HOW THEY DID IT

Most of these billionaires are business owners, and most of their gains were in the value of their stock. When their stock rises, they have "paper" gains, technically "unrealized" gains. There are no taxes on unrealized gains, and for good reason. Can you imagine the chaos if you were forced to pay taxes on the increase in the value of your home every year? People may be forced to sell their homes just to pay the taxes.

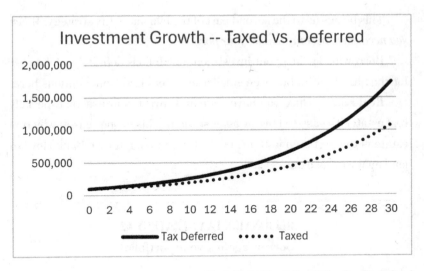

Figure 59: Investment Growth Taxed vs. Tax Deferred

When you sell an appreciated asset for a profit, you pay taxes on the profits. Because their taxes were so low, we can tell these billionaires didn't sell their stock.

This is the first part of the billionaire tax strategy: *Don't sell your appreciated investments.* One of the benefits of this strategy is that at your death all those capital gains are forgiven.

BILLIONAIRE TAX STRATEGY #1
Don't sell your appreciated investments.

But by doing that aren't you leaving a lot of equity trapped in your investments? Remember, using smart leverage is a key wealth-building strategy. What about accessing some of that equity to pay your bills or make new investments?

This brings us to the second part of the billionaire tax strategy: *When you need cash, borrow against your portfolio.*

Borrowing against your investment portfolio is definitely a lot easier for the ultrawealthy, but even smaller investors have some options here.

Real Estate. Once you have your first investment assets, especially real estate, it's easy to borrow against them. This is one reason why real estate is the first step in the Alts Continuum (chapter 5). Banks love to lend against real estate.

BILLIONAIRE TAX STRATEGY #2
Borrow against your portfolio.

Mortgage Debt. If you are just getting started, you may not have a real estate portfolio yet—but you still have options. An option available to many is household mortgage debt. If you have equity in your home, it's a simple matter to access that equity with a second mortgage or HELOC. Or even better, follow the strategies in the next chapter and open up a business loan with your home as collateral. I was able to obtain a business line of credit with a second mortgage on my home as collateral. The great thing about the line of credit is that it doesn't cost me anything if there is a zero balance. And I can borrow against it or pay it down as often as I like and only pay for what I am using. Plus, interest paid on a business loan (or mortgage debt on your primary residence) is also tax-deductible.

Margin Debt. Another option for many is margin debt. Margin debt is debt secured by your stocks and bonds portfolio. You can typically borrow up to 50 percent of the value of your portfolio, and most brokers offer a check-writing option. Margin debt has the advantage of being offered at lower interest rates. Also, interest paid on margin debt is tax-deductible if you have investment income.

Obviously, if you're going to use any of these debt strategies, use the smart debt principles laid out in #2.

Or Just Pay the Tax Man. Obviously debt comes with a price, and sometimes it's better to just pay the taxes. Long-term capital gains tax rates are low (15–20 percent), and paying them might be cheaper than leveraging for more than two to three years. Do the math, then decide.

CASH-OUT REFINANCE AND HOLD

One of the best ways to use the billionaire tax strategy is to simply *never sell your real estate*. Many real estate sponsors execute a value-add strategy, meaning they buy a property that needs some improvement in one way or another. Once it's improved, they can either sell it or refinance it at a higher value and take the cash out.

Here's how it works: Let's say you buy a $10 million apartment complex that needs a little renovation. You invest $3 million and borrow $7 million. You invest another $1 million to improve the property. Five years later, with your improved income, the property is now worth $15 million. Selling it would net you a profit of $4 million. But rather than sell it, you could refinance it, taking out a $10.5 million loan and putting a cool $3.5 million into your pocket to invest in new projects. You have your investment back, you still own the apartment complex, you will still have cash flow, and *you will pay no taxes on that transaction*.

REAL ESTATE TAX STRATEGIES: 1031 EXCHANGE AND DSTS

Real estate has a ton of tax benefits, and we are going to touch on them in this chapter.

One of the most popular is the 1031 exchange and its popular wrapper, the DST (Delaware Statutory Trust). Using a 1031 exchange, you can sell your property and defer your taxes by rolling it over into a new property or properties. There is no limit to how many times you can do this. There are also great estate-planning benefits, because when you die, your heirs do not have to pay all the deferred taxes.

But all these benefits come with some fairly hefty limitations:

- Intermediary: You must designate a special intermediary to receive the cash from the sale.
- The 45-day rule: You must designate the replacement property within 45 days of the sale. You can designate up to three possibilities as long as you close one of them.
- The 180-day rule: You must close on the new property within 180 days of the sale of the old property.
- Titling: Your new property and the old must be titled the same. This means that if the old property is held by you personally, the new property must also be. This limitation means that most of your passive investments (typically held as limited partnerships) don't qualify.

By now, you might be questioning the value of using 1031 exchanges to defer taxes. It's extremely difficult to find a property within 45 days and manage a very complicated transaction that includes the timing of the sale of the old property and the purchase of the new, especially if your preference is to be a passive versus active investor.

Delaware Statutory Trusts: A popular option that has emerged in the last few years is the Delaware Statutory Trust or DST. A DST is a real estate ownership structure that helps investors take advantage of 1031 exchange rules. In a DST, the trustee buys a property, and multiple investors each hold an *undivided fractional interest* in the property. That means your entity holds the property as a fractional owner.

Here's how it works: Let's say your investment entity, My Hub LLC, is selling a $1 million property. You find a DST sponsor who is offering interests in a multifamily property with a $25,000 minimum. You can invest from $25,000 up to the full $1 million. Your investment entity, My Hub LLC, will be named as a beneficiary of the trust along with the other investors. Taxes on the profit from the $1 million sale will be deferred. You can do this again and again, rolling profits from DST sales into new DST investments, and defer indefinitely. You can also invest in a DST without a previous sale to start the tax deferral when it exits.

DSTs have some advantages:

- DSTs are passive. The DST sponsors manage the property.
- DST sponsors typically offer professionally managed, institutional-quality real estate assets, including apartment complexes, industrial, office, and retail.
- DST sponsors can typically size your slice of the purchase to whatever you need. So it can precisely fit the size of the sale of your old property, or the exact amount of capital you want to deploy.

But the reality of 1031 exchanges and DSTs can be very ugly. To understand why, let's put ourselves in the shoes of a property sponsor for a moment. Let's say I have a $10 million apartment complex under contract to buy—why would I consider setting up a DST structure to purchase it? It would mean:

- Hefty legal fees and a very, very complicated transaction structure.
- A lengthy closing time frame that can be six months or longer.
- The stress and difficulty of finding a group of investors with just the right 1031 timing and amounts who like your project.

The reality is that no ordinary seller will agree readily to a six-month sale. And no sponsor will readily take on the expense and the risk of trying to cobble together a 1031 buyer pool. This leads to some inevitabilities:

- DST sponsors and the sellers of the properties they purchase are often *related parties*—the buying and selling entities share the same sponsor.
- Buyers typically overpay. The reason sellers are willing to take a six-month closing, and buyers are willing to embrace the headache, is because they are getting above-market prices.
- Fees are very rich. Layers of sellers, intermediaries, brokers, and sponsors all need to be paid. And because 1031 buyers are under the gun of the 45-day and 180-day rules, sponsors can take advantage with aggressive fees.

DSTs (but not non-DST 1031s) have other major limitations. The sponsor is not allowed to:
- Accept new capital after closing
- Renegotiate leases, terms, or enter into new leases
- Renegotiate debt terms or add debt
- Modify or improve the property

The debt, the leases, and the property must be completely set for the life of the DST. These limitations mean that only completely stabilized properties are suitable for DSTs. They typically hold high cash reserves and have low leverage, limiting the returns but reducing risk.

Because of all these factors, DSTs have lower returns. I have seen few I would be willing to invest in. For example, a typical non-DST multifamily investment may offer a 10–15 percent return. I don't think I have ever seen a DST multifamily investment return over 6 percent.

Don't be tax-smart and investment-stupid. Throughout my years working with investors, I have found a large percentage who are more concerned about avoiding taxes than making money. Make sure you run the numbers. If you can make a 15 percent IRR for five years and pay 20 percent capital gains tax, your after-tax IRR is 12.6 percent. It would be dumb to invest in DST with a 6 percent IRR. Go to investlikeabillionaire.org/book for a tax calculator to determine your own numbers.

If these are close to the numbers you are looking at, it's actually more advantageous to pay your taxes and invest in the higher-return, lower-risk non-1031 investment options.

Or use a "Lazy 1031."

ROLLING DEPRECIATION (THE LAZY 1031)

A far easier way to defer capital gains is to use rolling depreciation. Here's how it works.

Step 1: Sell your property toward the beginning of the calendar year. You will of course have a pending capital gains tax liability.

Step 2: Within the same calendar year, invest in a new purchase, making sure the sponsor does a "cost segregation study," to accelerate the depreciation schedule.

That's it. You don't have to worry about 1031 brokers, intermediaries, property matching, titling, or timing. It also works great with passive investments.

Most professional real estate sponsors will do cost segregation studies for new purchases. Because fixed assets have a fixed lifespan and must be replaced over time, the IRS allows you to depreciate them over their useful life. Things like HVAC units and roofs must all be replaced, and each has a different useful life. A cost segregation study calculates all these various lifespans and calculates the depreciation schedules. Different types of real estate have different levels of depreciation. Multifamily, for example, has higher levels of depreciation because it has more fixtures and appliances, which have faster depreciation schedules. Industrial real estate, with fewer depreciable components, has lower depreciation.

For some types of real estate, it's not uncommon to see depreciation in the range of 50–70 percent of your investment in the first year.

For example, if you invest $100,000, you will see $50,000 to $70,000 in depreciation that first year.

So, here's how it works for your tax situation. Let's say three years ago, you invested $100,000 in a property, and the sponsor is selling it this year. You expect to receive $180,000 from the sale and incur a capital gain of $80,000. You identify a new investment opportunity that has a 50 percent first-year depreciation. You invest $160,000 in that new deal and get an $80,000 first-year tax loss because of depreciation, offsetting the $80,000 gain. You have *zero tax liability from that sale in the current year*. The other benefit of this strategy is that when you purchase or invest in the new property, your "basis" gets reset, meaning any future capital gains will be based on the new investment amount, not the prior investment. This is the opposite of a 1031 exchange. When you sell a property, you have something called depreciation recapture, but you can usually repeat this process again and again and "defer until you drop."

A Lazy 1031 works because of something called "bonus depreciation." It allows you to accelerate your depreciation schedule, taking more depreciation in year one. Bonus depreciation has been in the tax code since 2002, and each time it is about to expire, Congress renews it again. Before relying on it, check the latest tax code to make sure it is still available.

In practice, a Lazy 1031 is actually very easy to do. When your sponsor is selling a property, you can estimate your capital gains. And when you find a new deal you like, ask the sponsor to estimate your first-year depreciation. Then do the math to figure out how much of the sale you should invest in the new deal. It's as simple as that.

This strategy also works for any capital gains. For example, you may have capital gains from selling appreciated stocks. Those can be easily offset using the above strategies.

I have also seen non-real estate private offerings that offer 100 percent bonus depreciation. One was an investment in a Bitcoin mining operation, the other an investment in ATM machines. Because the electronic hardware required depreciates very fast, they both offered first-year depreciation in the range of 90 percent. But keep in mind that these are non-real estate investments and have a higher risk.

A strong word of caution here: I have seen investors eagerly jump at real estate deals that offered over 100 percent first-year depreciation, but this is a major red flag. They offer such high depreciation by utilizing extreme leverage—as much as 90 percent. If you see a real estate investment with depreciation over 70 percent, make sure you do a deep dive on the cap table (see chapter 19) to see if it is over-leveraged.

Of all the tax strategies presented here, the Lazy 1031 has no downside, is very easy to execute, and can apply to almost everybody, including passive investors.

OPPORTUNITY ZONES

In 2017, Congress passed a law giving tax breaks for investment in "Opportunity Zones." These are specific geographic areas that are economically depressed or disadvantaged. Sponsors can form Opportunity Zone funds by simply investing 90 percent of the fund's capital into assets located in Opportunity Zones.

If held for ten years, investors incur no capital gains tax liability—literally all the profits are tax-free.

A secondary advantage is that if you invest capital gains dollars, those capital gains will be deferred through the year 2026. Of course, this means in 2026 all deferred gains will be due. At that point, you can use the "Lazy 1031" described above, or additional Opportunity Zone investments to defer again.

I have seen some great Opportunity Zone investments and have personally invested in several. But I have seen many more really lousy ones. Some of the worst ones I have seen were offered by broker-dealers and were clearly designed by the sponsors primarily as fee generators (see chapter 17).

You'll want to keep in mind that Opportunity Zone investments are made in or near depressed areas. This increases the risk profile, and you want to make sure you like the business plan, because the demographics will probably be entirely low-income. Of course, this is why the government is incentivizing these investments. But being in a low-income area doesn't necessarily unduly increase a project's risk.

ARE YOU A HIGH EARNER?

High earners (wage earners and business owners) have a real disadvantage in our tax system. This is the "ordinary income" bucket, and high earners pay the highest tax rates (currently as high as 37 percent). Furthermore, passive business losses, portfolio losses (like in stocks and bonds), and investment losses (like through depreciation mentioned above) can't reduce your ordinary income tax liability. To make matters worse, rental real estate is automatically considered passive income.

There is a hack, however, that can work for some people.

The trick is to become a Qualified Real Estate Professional (QREP). The good news is only one spouse needs to qualify for the tax benefits to apply to both of you. As a QREP, you can deduct real estate losses, like those easily generated through depreciation, against actively earned income—a huge plus. In addition, you also avoid the nasty 3.8 percent Net Investment Income Tax (NIIT) on portfolio income.

Practically, this means you or your spouse work in your real estate business fifteen hours per week. Here are the nitty-gritty details:

To be able to reduce active income with real estate losses, you must:
1. Qualify as a real estate professional, and
2. Materially participate in the rental property.
3. You qualify as a real estate professional if:
4. More than half of your personal services are in real property trades or businesses in which you materially participate; and

5. You perform more than 750 hours of services during the taxable year in real property trades or businesses in which you materially participate.

Tax law defines the term "real property trade or business" as any real property development, redevelopment, construction, reconstruction, acquisition, conversion, rental, operation, management, leasing, or brokerage trade or business.

For material participation, the regulations contain seven different tests.[63] Pass any one of the seven for a property, and you are deemed to materially participate in that property (unless you elected to include this property in a group).

OIL AND GAS WORKING INTERESTS

We covered oil and gas investing in detail in chapter 11, but let's briefly summarize some of the tax benefits here. Investment in oil and gas working interests is perhaps the most heavily incentivized activity in our tax code. It is missed by most investors because of reticence about the industry. But here are some of the advantages available if you choose to invest.

First is the depletion allowance. You only pay taxes on 85 percent of the earnings you make from oil and gas production. This is intended to compensate for the fact that an oil investment sees continuous depletion in its reserves. To take advantage of this, you don't need to do anything—it is automatic.

The second benefit is intangible drilling costs (IDCs). Whenever a new well is drilled, the intangible costs, which are the bulk of the costs incurred, are immediately tax-deductible. What's more, unlike real estate depreciation, IDCs are never recaptured. So any operation that includes steady drilling will have significant tax deductions.

Another huge advantage, especially for high earners—those with high salaries or business income—is that losses generated through IDCs can be used to reduce active income. In order to take advantage of this benefit, you must be a general partner (GP) in the investment. As a GP, you carry liability for the operation. Though it sounds very risky, in practice it is not. Well-run operators don't incur much liability and have insurance to cover any liabilities that do occur. Most sophisticated oil and gas sponsors will allow you to invest as a GP to take advantage of this if you choose. Most will also convert your investment from general partnership to limited partnership (which means you don't have any liabilities) after a period of time.

Again, a caution when investing in oil and gas. I have seen many offerings boasting 100 percent tax write-offs against active income. This is real, but it means that this company is planning on 100 percent new drilling to generate IDCs—a possibly very risky prospect. A smarter strategy is to invest in a blended offering—one that has producing assets generating income, as well as some new drilling to reduce the tax liabilities of that income and generate some tax benefits. However, it's possible that the income generated at the asset exceeds the losses, thereby not allowing those losses to pass through to offset other income or gains.

BALANCING YOUR INCOME BUCKETS

The US tax code (as well as most other nations) breaks your income down into three buckets:

- Active (wages and businesses you run)
- Passive (businesses you don't run, rental, real estate, and royalties)
- Portfolio (dividends, interest, and capital gains)

Losses in any one bucket cannot be used to offset gains in another. Depending on how you have earned your income, you may have gains in one bucket and disallowed losses in another. One strategy we love is to allocate your new investments in any calendar year to offset the gains and losses you expect in that year.

Practically, here's how you do it.

If you have high income in any bucket, look for ways to generate losses in that bucket. If you have losses in any bucket, look for ways to generate income in that bucket, which would be effectively tax-free for you. To get started, check your most recent tax return for where you stand in terms of your three buckets—you might need to get help from your tax professional here.

Active Income. Do you have lots of active income? Most high earners will find the bulk of your income here. This is one of the hardest situations to rectify, by design. But here are some things to consider:

- Shift your investments to generate more favorable income, like long-term capital gains and qualified dividends such as real estate.
- Become a qualified real estate professional as described above, and real estate losses can be counted as active losses.
- Invest in active oil and gas working interests that emphasize drilling, which can generate active losses. Remember that working interests can be active or passive. You must be prepared to take drilling risks.
- Maximize your IRAs, Solo 401(k)s, and cash balance plans (covered in the next chapter).
- Maximize the deductions in your investing business (also covered in the next chapter); consider buying an airplane!

Active Losses. Do you have active losses, called net operating losses (NOLs)? You are limited in the amount of NOLs you can deduct in any year, and the rest carry forward. Check your most recent tax return for disallowed NOLs, and if you have them, consider ways to get active income, like these:

- Increase your wages by consulting or doing gig work.

- Invest in active oil and gas working interests that emphasize production vs. drilling.
- Buy or start a business you help run. For example, I might partner with one of my children to run a short-term rental business, where I help choose the assets and oversee the finances while they do the rest, and we split the income.

Passive Income. Do you have lots of passive income? This is not common, and it is easy to offset passive income with passive losses. Consider:
- Investing in real estate, which will produce passive losses from depreciation.

Passive Losses. Do you have large passive activity losses (PALs)? This is very common, especially for anyone who has invested in real estate because of its depreciation. If this is you, consider:
- Investing in high-cash-flowing passive investments like rental real estate, royalties, private equity and passive, producing oil and gas working interests (again, working interests can be active or passive). This income will be tax-free until it exceeds your PALs. You should be aware that interest and dividend income is a special class of portfolio income that cannot be used to offset PALs.
- Liquidating a passive investment for gain, which will be tax-free until it exceeds your PALs.
- Become a QREP as described above, which would make your passive losses active.

Portfolio Gains. If you have large capital gains, consider:
- A 1031 exchange or a lazy 1031 as described above.
- Tax loss harvesting, selling losing positions to offset gains.

- Interest and dividend income is a special class of portfolio income that is taxed at high ordinary income rates. Consider placing interest producing investments like bonds and private credit to tax advantaged vehicles like IRAs and 401(k)s.

Portfolio Losses. If you have large capital losses, consider:
- Investing in capital gains producing investments like real estate and private equity.

CAUTION: TAX SHELTERS

It is amazing to me the lengths people will go to and the risks they will take to avoid paying taxes. I have seen investors eagerly pile into lousy investments to avoid paying modest taxes.

Here are some examples of some of the worst examples I have seen:
- 1031s and DSTs overpriced and loaded with fees just to avoid modest capital gains taxes.
- Opportunity Zone investments with lousy business plans and loaded with fees. Watch for "sales fees," which go to brokers. Remember that these brokers are getting paid for selling you this investment (see chapter 3).
- High-depreciation investments in real estate and non-real estate. Sometimes this depreciation is generated by using too much leverage, or because they are not real estate investments but investments in machinery.
- Oil and gas investments offering 90 percent tax deductions against active income. In other words, invest $100,000 and get a $90,000 deduction against W-2 income. The problem is that the only way to do this is to drill. It means this investment is a drilling play—they plan on spending all your investment capital drilling new wells. Make sure you understand those risks.

I recently saw an investment offering pitch that led with its tax benefits. This is a major red flag. Never choose an investment primarily because of its tax benefits. Never let the tax tail wag your investment dog!

> **Never let the tax tail wag your investment dog!**

Bottom line: There are plenty of lousy investments out there, many marketed for their tax benefits. Sometimes, it's better just to pay the taxes and make great investments. Don't make a lousy investment, period—you don't need to.

On the other hand, some of these tax strategies are simply fantastic! They don't require a lot of effort, and as long as you choose great sponsors and great projects, they have no downside. These include:
- Cash-out refinance and hold strategies.
- Rolling depreciation (Lazy 1031) strategies.
- Opportunity Zone investments.
- Balancing your income buckets.
- Oil and gas investments.
- And best of all, making everything a business.

MAKE EVERYTHING A BUSINESS—INCLUDING YOUR FUN

Before we hit our last tax strategy, do this: Schedule a call with your tax professional to discuss your tax strategy, and do it early in the year when you have time to act on it. Have them look at your active, passive, and portfolio income, as well as any carryforwards, to know how you need to best allocate future investments.

The final strategy is my personal favorite: Turn everything into a business, including your fun! Investing doesn't have to be dull and boring; it can be a blast!

And your fun investment business can generate huge tax benefits as well.

In the next chapter, we'll show you how.

CHAPTER 14

ORGANIZING AND STRUCTURING YOUR INVESTMENTS

"An idiot with a plan can beat a genius without a plan."
- Warren Buffett

Before you progress very far on your private alternatives journey, one question that is sure to arise is: How do I structure my investment holdings? Most investors just begin by investing in their own name. This is a huge mistake! Before you go very far, you should set up our preferred structure: the hub LLC.

It begins with an important mindset shift. You should think of your investment journey not as "making some investments," but as an *investment business*. This is a real business you are spending time and money on, learning and growing and improving your skills, and getting professional advice. Your hub LLC is your investment business.

MINDSET SHIFT #6
Treat your investments as a business.

It's very easy to set up and will give you a number of great benefits.

If you are single, it will be a single member LLC. If you are married, you should set it up with yourself and your spouse as the members (or better yet, your trusts) both owning 50 percent of the shares. You might have a family trust, which should be the single owner of the LLC.

GETTING STARTED

Creating your hub LLC is just a quick call to your attorney, or just a few simple steps if you want to do it yourself:

1. Draft a simple member-managed operating agreement. You can use an online legal website to save money, but I recommend hiring an attorney. It should only cost a few hundred dollars.
2. Go to the Secretary of State website for the state where you live and register a new LLC. You can typically do this online for less than $100.
3. Go to the IRS website and file for a federal EIN (employer identification number). This is your IRS tax ID.
4. With these three items, you can go to any bank and open a bank account. You're in business!
5. Finally, open up a business credit card. American Express, Chase, and Capital One all have great options. Capital One reports to your personal credit, which can be a positive if you are trying to build it. Chase and American Express do not. You can decide which is better for your personal situation.

You can freely move money in and out of your hub LLC. When you put money in, it's called an owner's contribution. When you pull money out, it's called an owner's draw. Neither has tax consequences.

It's important to remember not to commingle funds. This means to be sure to use your business credit card and business checking account only for business expenses—don't treat them as your personal accounts. If you do, you risk voiding all the benefits of your hub LLC.

Using Your Hub LLC to Invest

As soon as your hub LLC is set up, all investments you make should be titled in the name of the hub LLC. For example, your hub LLC might be called "My Hub LLC." When you invest, ask for your investment to be titled in the name of "My Hub LLC." Your hub LLC qualifies as an accredited investor if all the members are accredited—i.e., you (or you and your spouse).

Estate Planning

The hub LLC is part of a well-designed estate plan. If you are single, you would own 100 percent of this LLC. Because it is a single member LLC, it would be considered a disregarded entity by the IRS, and the business would not file its own tax return; its activity would appear directly on your personal tax return on Schedule C.

If you are married, a common structure is to have the hub LLC owned by you and your spouse 50 percent each. In this case, the hub LLC would file its own tax return, which is actually a benefit.

Either way, a common structure in estate plans is just to set up a personal revocable trust. If you are married, you would both have such a trust. You might also have a family trust for the two of you. This trust (or trusts) will be the actual owner(s) of the LLC. This structure allows maximum benefit to you as an investment business owner and your spouse after you die. It avoids probate and has several other significant benefits. It's beyond the scope of this book to consider estate planning. Consult your attorney for more information and structuring details.

Combining Your Business Activities

For years, I have run a small authoring and speaking business. While rewarding, publishing has not always produced much income. Without the supporting income, you can't take advantage of most of the tax benefits like expense deductions, Solo 401(k)s, etc. In addition, any business that runs multiyear deficits could be classified by the IRS as a hobby and be disqualified as a real business, especially if it's sitting on your personal tax return as a loss on your Schedule C.

By combining everything into my investment business, I have a single business that encompasses all my activities. For me, it's an investing/authoring/speaking business. When combined, the business as a whole runs a profit. Your profits allow you to deduct travel; own and deduct equipment, airplanes and automobiles; set up Solo 401(k)s, etc. And if you are co-owners with your spouse, traveling together for business is all deductible.

If you have multiple businesses that cannot be combined, create a consulting agreement from your other businesses to your hub LLC. In this way, you can deduct business expenses from all of your business activities in one place—your hub LLC. For example, let's say your hub LLC is My Hub LLC. You also own Company A separately. Company A hires My Hub LLC as a consultant for $10,000 per month. Now My Hub LLC can travel (and deduct expenses) on behalf of its investment business, its speaking/authoring activities, as well as all Company A activities.

Expenses

You may be surprised at the things you are able to deduct. According to the IRS, all business expenses must meet two criteria to qualify as business expenses.

1. **Ordinary:** This means it's typical in your business, both in terms of amount as well as in frequency and purpose.
2. **Necessary:** This means it helps you increase your profits or expand your business.

Some of the expenses you can deduct:

- All your subscriptions that help you be a better investor, like the *Wall Street Journal*, and other online services
- Conferences you attend that might help you in your investing business
- Masterminds that help grow your business
- Storage used for business
- Home office use
- Business telephone use, according to the percentage of business use
- Computer and office equipment used more than 50 percent of the time for business
- Business travel

Travel

For travel to be deductible, it must pass these four tests.

For starters, your trip must have a business purpose, meaning it must include activities such as client meetings, attending a conference, being a guest speaker at a conference, doing research and development for the business, or holding a board meeting or annual shareholders' meeting. The activity should have the potential to generate revenue.

> To be tax-deductible, travel activities should have the potential to generate revenue.

"Don't think you can take a personal trip, talk business for an hour, and then try and deduct the whole amount of your trip. The intent of the trip needs to be business," says Caitlynn Eldridge, founder and CEO of Eldridge CPA.[64]

The second and third requirements deem that the trip must be both "ordinary and necessary," according to IRS guidelines on business travel expenses. "An ordinary expense means it's typical in your business, both in terms of amount as well as in frequency and purpose. Necessary means it actually helps you increase your profits or expand your business," explains Tom Wheelwright, a certified public accountant and author of the book *Tax-Free Wealth*.[65]

Lastly, every expense must be properly documented. To get a deduction for travel, Wheelwright said that you must spend more than half your time during the business day doing business and have everything documented. "So, if you spend four and a half hours a day doing business, it becomes deductible. You also must have documentation, which includes receipts, of what you did, and a log of your expenses," says Wheelwright.

On receipts, write the name of the client who you had the meal with for further proof. "Save the emailed confirmation and receipt from the hotel reservation or conference ticket payment that show the dates, times, and name of the events as well as the receipts from the travel it took to get there and back (such as for gas or flights)," says Ben Watson, founder of Fiscal Fluency, a personal finance and business coaching company.[66]

Know, too, that you must be away from home overnight—the IRS requires an overnight stay for the trip to qualify as business travel, Wheelwright says.

Solo 401(k)

One of the greatest benefits of having an investment business is that you are now *self-employed* (even if you have a full-time job), and that means you can set up a Solo 401(k). Most people know what a 401(k) is—a tax-deferred savings program you can contribute capital to. The Solo 401(k) is a supercharged version for the self-employed, allowing you and to contribute up to $76,500 per year in tax-deferred investment. If you co-own the investment business with your spouse, you can both defer up to $76,500 per year.

This is a fantastic opportunity to help you grow your wealth. They were conceived as a way to help self-employed people build for retirement, because presumably they don't have a corporate pension program.

There are a few limitations to keep in mind:

- To qualify for a Solo 401(k), your business must have no employees, and just one owner plus a spouse if they also work for the business—which is perfect for your investment business.
- You may open a Solo 401(k) even if you are also participating in your employer's 401(k). However, your contribution limits apply to all 401(k) contributions combined. Make sure to consult an attorney or tax advisor.
- Your business can contribute 25 percent of its profits to your Solo 401(k)s up to a maximum of $46,000 for each spouse. You are also allowed to contribute individually 100 percent of your business income up to $23,000 (or $30,500 if you are over 50), for a total of up to $76,500 each.
- Your business contributions must go into a traditional plan, and your individual contributions can go into a traditional or Roth plan. Some 401(k) providers will limit your choices here.
- Traditional funds are tax-deductible the year you make the contribution, grow tax-free, and are taxed when you withdraw them.
- Roth funds are not tax-deductible, grow tax-free, and are not taxed on withdrawal if you are 59½ and have had your account for five years.
- You can convert Traditional funds to Roth funds at any time. You will pay tax on the conversion amount.

Your Solo 401(k) also can be self-directed—meaning you can use the funds to invest in private alternatives as well.

You will need to find a Solo 401(k) provider. You open the accounts and then fund them from your business and personal accounts. You can then access that cash to make tax-free (Roth) or tax-deferred (Traditional) investments. If it is self-directed, you can direct them to make the private alts investments you choose.

You might be familiar with IRAs and Self-directed IRAs, Solo 401(k)s are similar but far more powerful:

1. You can contribute much larger amounts of capital.
2. Solo 401(k)s are exempt from UDFI tax. Many alternative investments are leveraged with debt. Most IRA investors are shocked to find out that their "tax-free" IRAs must actually pay UDFI tax on profits from leveraged investments! However, Solo 401(k)s do not pay this tax, making them ideal for investing in private alts.
3. IRAs aren't available for high earners, but Solo 401(k)s have no income limits.
4. Borrowing is not allowed from your IRA but is allowed from your Solo 401(k) if your provider supports it.

Once you have your Solo 401(k) account open, you should transfer your Traditional IRAs into them for this reason. You are not allowed to transfer your Roth IRA to your Solo 401(k).

A smart timing strategy can also save you a ton of money. If your taxable income varies a lot, I recommend keeping both a Roth and a Traditional 401(k). When your income is high, contribute to your Traditional for the tax deduction. If you have a lower-income year and drop to a lower tax bracket, transfer some money from your Traditional to your Roth. You will owe income tax on the amount of the transfer but pay less in taxes because your rate is lower. I was able to use this strategy to make a large transfer from Traditional to Roth tax-free—a silver lining in an otherwise bad year.

Solo 401(k)s are also protected from creditors and bankruptcy. The advantages keep on going!

Solo 401(k)s also allow penalty-free hardship withdrawals for essential medical expenses for treatment and care, home-buying expenses for a principal residence, educational tuition and fees, expenses to prevent being foreclosed on or evicted, and more.

The Cash Balance Pension Plan

Want to defer even more? The lesser-known cash balance plan is also a favorite of the self-employed.

401(k)s are defined *contribution* plans, while cash balance plans are defined *benefit* plans. The idea is that you define a benefit amount you would like to receive at retirement, and you contribute toward that every year. The maximum benefit is large, up to $3.4 million and growing every year.

Contribution limits can also be large, depending on your age. Since the idea is to get you $3.4 million at retirement, the older you are the more you must contribute to get there. The amount can be as high as $376,000 for a 66-year-old. Combined with a Solo 401(k), your tax-deferred contribution would total $452,000.

Roth versions are not permitted. Proceeds grow at a fixed interest rate every year tax-free, and distributions are taxed. Self-direction is not allowed.

You may also roll the funds into a Traditional Solo 401(k) or IRA when the plan ends.

For a current list of 401(k) providers we like, visit investlikeabillionaire.org/book.

Liability Protection

The final advantage of a hub LLC is liability protection. If someone sues one of your businesses or investment properties, you are personally protected from liability. It's wise to go even further, putting every property in its own LLC, wholly owned by your hub LLC. A single member LLC is a disregarded entity, which means it does not file a tax return. But it does provide liability protection. It means a lawsuit at one property does not endanger any of your other investments in your hub LLC.

So now you know how to structure your investments. Next, let's look at how smart investors choose their investments.

CHAPTER 15

BUILDING A SMART PORTFOLIO

"Money is like manure. You have to spread it around, or it smells."
- J. Paul Getty

This chapter, along with the next, will be the two most important in determining your success as an alts investor. Data shows that success hinges almost entirely on two factors: *your allocation strategy* and your *sponsor selection*s. Careful attention and discipline in these two areas will give you an excellent chance of outperforming results.

David Swensen argued that your allocation strategy was the greatest factor driving investors' results.[67] Fortunately, it is not difficult!

Most investors start investing more or less randomly, picking whatever they come across—what a friend invested in, a family member, something you stumbled upon. But this is not how the ultrawealthy invest! Think about David, who found himself day one with a billion-dollar portfolio. He didn't just start putting money in whatever he came across. He first formulated a plan of how he wanted to allocate those funds.

Here we have another key mindset shift: Before you invest, plan your allocation strategy. You must first intentionally and proactively choose how you want to invest. In this chapter, we will help you formulate your allocation strategy.

MINDSET SHIFT #7

Before investing, plan your allocation strategy.

LIQUIDITY

When building your Billionaire Portfolio Allocation, the first thing to consider is your liquidity need, which most investors overestimate. Instead, let's take the time to calculate it.

First, think about your personal needs, the things you might need cash for in the next three to five years, like:

1. A cushion for a lost job _____
2. Replacing an aging car _____
3. Sending a child to college _____
4. Purchasing a property _____
5. Starting a business _____
6. Other _____

Next, think about your existing investments. Are there any possible capital calls that could come? What about your business—what would be its cash needs in a pinch? Warren Buffet said, "Investors should avoid behavior that could result in any uncomfortable cash needs at inconvenient times, including financial panics."[68] Wise advice! Let's add these:

7. Possible cash needs for investments _____
8. Possible cash needs for business _____
9. Total _____

Adding up all these, you now have your liquidity need. There are three ways to meet this liquidity need.

Cash. Cash is the most expensive option for liquidity—expensive in that it earns you very little, usually below the level of inflation. The ultrawealthy allocate 5–10 percent to cash.

Bonds. Bonds are a highly liquid and efficient market. You can buy and sell them quickly, easily, and cheaply. Bonds earn low returns but are uncorrelated to stocks and can also count against your liquidity need. The ultrawealthy invest 5–10 percent in bonds.

Lines of Credit. Having too much in cash and bonds can hurt your returns. Debt, specifically lines of credit, can help meet your liquidity need without forcing you too heavily into cash and bonds. Yale developed what they called "sources of non-disruptive liquidity" that they could access without forcing them to sell anything.[69] They obtained a $2 billion line of credit, secured by their portfolio. Lines of credit generally cost little or nothing and can count toward your liquidity need.

There is an easy line of credit everyone can get: a stock market margin loan. Most stockbrokers will give you a line of credit for up to 50 percent of your public market portfolio. You should also consider putting in place other lines of credit—for example, against your real estate or business.

You might be tempted to count your public equities portfolio against your liquidity need. I would advise against it; accessing it could mean being forced to sell at a loss in a market panic.

THE BILLIONAIRE PORTFOLIO ALLOCATION

Let's construct your Billionaire Portfolio Allocation. You already have your all-important cash and bonds component.

Next, consider your public equities portfolio. The ultrawealthy invest 20–30 percent here, but there is no "right" answer. Balance your desire to own the world's best companies, and boost secondary liquidity, against volatility.

Now, for your private alternatives. Choose three to five investment asset classes. These are your investment "buckets." Use the Alts Continuum (p. 81) as a guide.

Finally, choose the size of each bucket as a percentage of the total.

To get you started, we have constructed example portfolios based on how the ultrawealthy invest and the size of your investable capital—the *Billionaire Portfolio Allocation*.

The Billionaire Portfolio Allocation			
Asset Class	Your Investable Capital		
	$1 mil.	$10 mil.	$100 mil.
Cash	10%	10%	5%
Bonds	15%	10%	5%
Public Equities	35%	30%	20%
Private Real Estate	30%	25%	20%
Private Credit	5%	10%	15%
Energy / Natural Resources / Infrastructure	5%	10%	15%
Private Equity / Venture Capital / Hedge Funds	0%	5%	20%

Feel free to modify this table to your own personal needs and desires. Add your favorite investment classes like crypto, gold, currencies, life insurance, absolute return, or infrastructure. In studying the portfolios of the ultrawealthy, I have found a lot of variation in portfolio construction—there is no single "perfect" or "correct" way to invest. The point of having a target allocation is just to help you build a portfolio of truly uncorrelated assets and avoid overinvestment in a single asset class.

Now, let's look in detail at this table.

If you have $1 million or less to invest, you probably already have most of your investment capital in the stock market. That's fine! There is no need to make big, sudden moves. Over time, as you choose investments, simply fill the buckets that have room while gradually divesting the ones that are overfilled.

The first asset class to fill in is real estate (chapter 6). Real estate is the first step in the Alts Continuum, and for good reason. It is the easiest to access, it is understandable, and it has lots of benefits.

You should also consider some investments in private credit and natural resources—private credit (chapter 7) for its safety and income potential, and natural resources (chapter 11) for its income and strongly uncorrelated behavior.

As your investment portfolio grows, you will typically move up the Alts Continuum into more "exotic" investments like private equity, venture capital, and hedge funds.

As you consider your allocation strategy, keep David Swensen's advice in mind. He believed that if you have a longer time horizon, you should focus primarily on equity investments (public equities, real estate, private equity, and venture capital) and accept the risk. He noted that in the years 1925–2009, Treasury bills returned a total of 21x (9x after counting inflation), bonds 86x, but stocks 2,592x, and small stocks 12,226x, even including the 90 percent drop between 1929 and 1932.[70] You should emphasize equity classes as much as your time horizon and your need for income can tolerate.

REBALANCING

We covered rebalancing your public equities portfolio in chapter 12, but how do you handle rebalancing an alts-heavy portfolio? Alts are more challenging because generally they don't have liquidity, so selling is not an option.

1. Rebalance your public equities and bonds holdings annually.
2. Whenever you have an exit in your alts portfolio, rebalance again, this time your overall portfolio.
3. Finally, allocate new capital to buckets that are below target.

Trapped! Business Owners & 401(k) Owners

Many investors find themselves trapped in large investment positions. For example, you might own a large stock position in the company you work for; or you have grown a sizable 401(k) that is stuck in mutual funds; or you own a successful business that has most of your capital. What do you do?

Treat that oversized investment as a bucket in which you are overinvested, like this:

Asset Class	Current Allocation	Target Allocation
My Company or 401(k)	90%	30%
Everything Else—Your Billionaire Portfolio Allocation	10%	70%

Realize that you are overinvested in one thing and work diligently to diversify. Divert income from your business, partially divest when you can, or borrow against your large holdings, then invest the cash in other asset classes.

"I Just Got $57 Million! What Do I Do?"

I was sitting with a friend when he got this urgent text message: "I just got $57 million! What do I do?" We laughed together as we knew this guy was going to be making some boneheaded mistakes in his urgency to deploy his cash. But how *do* you handle a big windfall like a successful business exit?

Most importantly, resist the urge to start investing rapidly. Design your ideal portfolio allocation and set a long-time horizon, such as five years, to achieve it. This will keep you from jumping on this year's investment fads and ending up fully invested when next year's best opportunities roll around.

FILLING YOUR BUCKETS

As you construct your portfolio, here are some important principles to remember.

Don't Overinvest in a Bucket. Once the bucket is full, be disciplined. Even if some great deals come along, you should consider whether it's worth being overallocated.

Don't Invest More Than 5 percent in Any Single Deal. This can be tough, especially when you fall in love with a deal like I do! But remember your discipline. Investing 5 percent in a deal means that if it happens to lose 50 percent of its value, it only hurts your portfolio by 2.5 percent.

> Don't invest more than 5 percent in any single deal.

Under no circumstances should you put more than 10 percent of your investable assets into a single deal. This is making "the bet"—it's like putting all your chips on one number in roulette.

Choose Uncorrelated Assets Within the Buckets. Remember one of the most important lessons of this book: *Portfolio volatility is less than average volatility if the assets are uncorrelated* (chapter 4). By following your Billionaire Portfolio Allocation, you will be diversified in the biggest sense. But you can also further diversify by consciously choosing assets that are individually uncorrelated from each other. For example, in your real estate bucket, further diversify by choosing different classes of real estate, like multifamily, industrial, and retail.

Diversify Geographically. You can also diversify by selecting different geographies. For several years, investing in "Sun Belt" real estate was the rage. A few years later, Sun Belt properties had become dramatically overbuilt and were struggling, while previously boring Midwest and "Rust Belt" states were far outperforming. While I strongly advocate paying attention to megatrends, every trend will eventually change, and you should always hedge your bets.

Diversify Operators. As you advance on your investment journey, you will inevitably find operators you love. As tempting as it might be to put everything on the proven players you know, you should diversify even there. Leadership changes, culture changes, key employee losses, a regulatory hit, a lawsuit, or a public controversy can all derail an operator. (We'll say more about operators in our next chapter.)

THE IMPORTANCE OF MEGATRENDS

I have personally experienced the drama of four decades of investment cycles, a half dozen crashes and crises, and at least as many booms. It certainly gives you some perspective! One of the most personal for me was the dot-com era. I was a dot-com founder, raising $44 million in venture capital and growing the business up to nearly three hundred employees.

Just as we were readying our IPO, the dot-com crash wiped us out. I lost everything.

It was a defining moment for me. I became passionate about studying macroeconomics, trends, and data. I had always read up on these topics, but now it became an obsession. Today I read and study for hours every day to *understand the forces at work*.

I began to make forecasts, including some wrong calls which I learned from, but also a lot of good ones—the gold boom of the 2000s to currency crashes and the strong dollar trend; investment opportunities in real estate during past crises, such as the S&L collapse and the Great Financial Crisis—and advised buying at key market bottoms. I also anticipated broader economic trends, including the US reshoring movement, energy booms, and shifting inflationary cycles.

When I say I "called" them, I mean that *I correctly identified the forces at work, their importance, and their net effects*. I call these *tides*. Tides are big trends, usually decades in the making, driven by very large, but often slow-moving economic forces.

What I rarely did, and what is nearly impossible to do, is forecast *the precise top or bottom, or timing* of these outcomes. When my timing happened to be right, it was luck.

What else is impossible is predicting the movement of the stock market, or housing prices, or currencies or commodities this month or year, or what the Federal Reserve will do. I call these *waves*.

Waves are unpredictable, but the tides are very predictable.

In 2012, based on the tides, we started investing in distressed real estate debt and made nearly high-teens returns for almost a decade.

What I try to do is identify the tides. I do it to find an edge in my investing. Investing opportunistically with the megatrends can increase your returns to the higher end of the spectrum. Instead of 10–15 percent returns, you might be able to get 15–20+ percent returns over short periods of time.

The idea is not to replace your portfolio allocation methodology described above, but to *inform* it. I use megatrends in two ways: first, in selecting the particular investments within an asset class; and second, to adjust allocations slightly in favor of my preferred investments. For example, by increasing an allocation to oil and gas by 5 percent, or shifting an allocation to industrial real estate to play the reshoring trend. Even if I get the trend wrong, I still have a solid investment, and my Billionaire Portfolio Allocation is still working for me—so it doesn't hurt me. But making correct calls can materially enhance your returns.

We invest extraordinary time and effort to research the biggest trends to develop our internal investing playbook. We also freely share our playbook on our podcast, *Invest Like a Billionaire*, at thebillionairepodcast.com.

THE OTHER HIDDEN REWARD

Following these simple allocation guidelines will have a great payoff for you. We have talked extensively about higher returns with lower risk and lower volatility. One other reward is peace of mind. I remember my days as a professional trader, when sometimes the entire screen goes red, giving me a giant pit in my stomach! Following these models, those days are long gone. David Swensen put it like this:

> So, one of the great things about having a diversified portfolio is that you can worry less about the relative level of valuation of various assets in which you invest. So, if you go back to the mid-'80s and you've got a portfolio that's 50% in domestic stocks, you have to worry a lot about the valuation of that portfolio, because half of your assets are in that single asset class. But if you've got a well-diversified portfolio with, let's say, minimum allocation of 5 to 10%, and now a maximum allocation of 25 to 30% in an individual asset class, the relative valuation of each of those asset classes matters less.[71]

So, you know how to construct a portfolio. In the next chapter, we will learn about the single greatest factor that will determine your success investing in private alts.

CHAPTER 16

HOW TO SELECT AN OPERATOR

"Is there such thing as a cheerful pessimist? That's what I am."
- Charlie Munger

After your initial decision to invest in private alts, choosing an operator will have more impact on your success than any other. Recall *Figure 18: Public and Private Manager Dispersion* (p. 71). Let's take a closer look at this data. In the real estate sector, the best managers of public core real estate generated 7.3 percent returns, and the worst 5.8 percent. That's not very much difference.

But look at the managers of *private* non-core real estate. The best managers generated 13.6 percent returns—double their public counterparts—and the worst -3 percent.

There are two things you should catch here. First, the best *private operators doubled the returns seen by the public managers.* The data sampled was from a slightly riskier asset class (non-core), but still, that should wake you up! How is this possible? Because of all the factors mentioned in chapter 5, "What Makes Private Alts So Attractive:" low volatility, tax advantages, niche opportunities, lower regulation, and so on.

The second takeaway you should note is the vast difference between the best operators and the worst. While the best doubled the returns of public managers, the worst *lost money*.

It is possible, through your selection of operators, *to deliver results that far outpace anything possible in the public markets*. It is also possible to do *far worse*. Looking more closely, it's even more extreme. The chart shows only the second and third quartiles—so 25 percent of managers did even *better* than shown, and 25 percent *worse*.

It is precisely this challenge that gives many investors pause, but we'll show you some of the ways to mitigate these risks and select great operators. While it takes an investment of time, it is not difficult and will have a game-changing payback. It is also the primary way you, the individual investor, can distinguish yourself from your peers

START WITH A "NO" WHILE LOOKING FOR A "YES"

Because you are reading a book like this, you are probably an optimist. Beware, optimism could be deadly to you as an investor! You will be talking to great salesmen, and if your default disposition is a yes you are destined to invest in some real stinkers. Flip the script! Assume every deal is a bad one, and invest only when it checks all the boxes. Early on, especially, you will be itchy to place capital. Resist the urge and be patient. Be very, very, very selective. Here are some tips for starting out:

1. When you start evaluating a deal, assume it is problematic and not a fit for you. Expect it will be a no
2. Resolve in your mind to be heavily in cash for a while.
3. For your first dozen alts investments, place minimal capital no matter how great you think a deal is.
4. For your first deal with a new sponsor, place minimal capital.

I admit I violated every one of these principles starting out. I ended up with a pile of dogs in my portfolio and cash poor when the really good deals came around. Ugh! All of my worst deals were my first deals. Hopefully you can learn from my experience and not have to make these mistakes for yourself!

I love Warren Buffet's comments on the temperament required to be a successful investor:

> The [investors] that have the edge are the ones who really have the temperament to look at a business, look at an industry and not care what the person next to them thinks about it, not care what they read about it in the newspaper, not care what they hear about it on the television, not listen to people who say, "This is going to happen," or, "That's going to happen."
>
> You have to come to your own conclusions, and you have to do it based on facts that are available. If you don't have enough facts to reach a conclusion, you forget it. You go on to the next one. You have to also have the willingness to walk away from things that other people think are very simple.
>
> Temperament's important.[72]

HOW NOT TO SELECT AN OPERATOR

Inexperienced investors make a number of common mistakes when selecting operators. Here are a few:

1. **Focusing on "the deal" instead of the operator.** While the deal may capture your attention, at the end of the day, every deal is just a set of promises. And promises are only as good as the promiser.
2. **Focusing on headline returns.** New investors always gravitate toward bigger projected returns—which, again, are just claims. How solid is their business plan? What are the risks? The liquidity and timing? Do they have a track record?

3. **Locking on to the first operator encountered.** It's called availability bias—our brains latch on to the first option we hear about. Don't do it—go "shopping."
4. **Following the crowd.** Humans are wired to get confidence and comfort from others. Make your own decisions.
5. **Getting operator referrals from unsophisticated investors.** Your neighbor, or brother-in-law, your lawyer, and your CPA might be smart, but if they aren't individually, personally successful private alts investors, their advice is best ignored! I'll say it again—ignore it! I have consistently found that some of the smartest people—doctors, lawyers, academics, etc.—start out as the *worst investors*. Humans are wired to trust "experts," but if they are not successful alts investors, don't even bother to ask their opinions.

REFERRALS

When getting started, selecting operators can be a daunting task. There are literally tens of thousands of operators, all with compelling pitches. The best way to get started is to network with experienced, successful private alts investors.

> **The best way to get started is to network with experienced, successful private alts investors.**

Find experienced, savvy investors who don't just talk about headline returns but talk about risk and risk-adjusted returns, diversification, and operator intangibles like excellence, communication, doing what they say, and transparency.

The way to find experienced investors is through investment events, investor clubs, and investor masterminds. For a current list of masterminds and conferences we like, visit investlikeabillionaire.org/book.

CO-INVESTMENT

If you only review one area, co-investment should be the one—how much of their own capital is the sponsor putting in the deal? This is perhaps the single most important factor in selecting an operator. You want to know that your operator has significant personal capital at stake alongside yours. Any operator dodging this question or not investing materially raises a red flag. David Swensen echoed the same sentiment: "A high level of co-investment by the general partner represents a sure way to align investor interests."[73] In fact, in his book, Swensen mentioned co-investment thirty-two times.

This is a very important metric because, as we have seen, sponsors always share the upside of the project, and in that way, your interests are aligned. But unless the sponsor also has their own capital at stake in the deal, *they do not share the downside risk* with you. You want a sponsor that shares in both the upside and the downside, and only then can you be assured your interests are truly aligned.

> Unless the sponsor also has their own capital at stake in the deal, they do not share the downside risk with you.

Some sponsors can be more fee driven than investor driven. Fees are normal and necessary. However, the more reliant sponsors become on fees, especially up-front or maintenance fees, the more they can become fee driven. One of the easiest ways to tell the difference is how much co-investment they are making in the deal. In our firm, Aspen Funds, we commit that every partner invests materially in every deal we sponsor, and on the same terms as our investors. One of our younger partners eagerly takes all his excess cash and places it in every deal. Another firm I'm aware of touts that their founders have invested $80 million of their personal capital into their funds.

This gives you a lot of confidence that your interests are aligned in several ways:
1. The operator is focused on the performance of the asset as much as you are.
2. They are not going to lose focus and get too busy doing something else.
3. They will fight for the success of a deal when things get tough.

I recall a couple of cases where I violated this principle as an investor. One was a Bitcoin mining fund. There were a lot of red flags, but I invested anyway because I liked the space. The operator was intelligent and focused but had no co-investment and took 50 percent of the profits as fees. When the Bitcoin mining world later encountered serious economic challenges, he simply walked away and left investors without a manager. His upside gone, and no downside to protect—it cost him nothing. Had he tried, he could easily have recovered investors' capital, but his exit resulted in 100 percent losses. Had he made a large co-investment, he never would have walked away like that.

TRACK RECORD

If there are only two areas you review, the second should be an operator's track record. Financial disclosures are famous for saying "past performance does not guarantee future results." And while that's certainly true, past performance *matters*. It might indeed be an indicator of luck, but it can also be an indicator of your operator's skill—it's up to you to decide which.

Eliminate Luck. When reviewing the entire track record, filter out the results where clearly luck was involved. During the dot-com boom of the late 1990s, every dot-com soared in value, and if your operator was in that space at that time, luck played a larger part than skill in their success. Similarly, anyone who sold commercial real estate in the COVID boom of 2021 and 2022 was lucky. Eliminate them as valid data points. Look at how their investments performed in difficult times, like:

- in recessions like the Great Recession of 2007–2009
- in shocks like the COVID shock of 2020–2021
- when interest rates rise rapidly as in 2022–2023

Ask about their worst deal and how they managed it. Keep in mind that every operator with a long enough history will encounter adversity. You are not looking for perfection or psychic foresight, but for honesty, smarts, agility, and someone who will fight like hell for their investors when things get tough. For example, in my firm when one of our deals soured, we upped our efforts and dropped all our fees.

> **The way to find experienced investors is investment events, investor clubs, and investor masterminds.**

You don't have to be an economic genius to identify lucky results. When reviewing their track record, ask the operator where luck was involved.

Beware of Selective Track Record Presentations. Ask for the operator's entire track record. Many operators will show only their best results. Make sure you see the entire track record. Ask about their worst deals and what they learned from those deals. Anyone who is not forthcoming should be passed on. You will learn a lot about them, and also about the markets you are investing in.

SIZE MATTERS

In operator selection, size matters. Many of the poorest deals I have done personally were with operators that were too small. Smaller operators can easily get overextended. They often don't have the team to execute best practices in asset selection, underwriting, asset management, back-office operations, or reporting. They don't get access to the best deals. They don't have robust and fully developed systems and processes in place. They are often dependent upon one guy, and can be autocratic, lacking in the wisdom of a diversified team.

If I am investing $100,000, I want to see an operator who has managed at least $25 million in investor capital. Beware of looking at statistics like assets under management (AUM), which can present inflated numbers. If you are a larger investor, you generally want to work with even larger operators. If you do choose to work with smaller operators, just make smaller allocations.

Size isn't always a perfect indicator. One of my favorite operators is a small firm we have worked with on retail real estate investments. Their smarts and skills are incredibly impressive. They have great back-office support, staff, systems, and processes in place. Their principal has over a decade of experience working in their space.

On the other hand, I've worked with a large operator with an impressive team and track record in the self-storage space. Due to their aggressive growth goals, they overcommitted their staff to too many competing deals. They missed their key timelines to put permanent financing in place and were forced to take debt on very unfavorable terms. As a result, the investment is underperforming. The good news is that while it's not cash-flowing very well, we still expect to do well upon exit. That's one of the great things about real estate investment: Even with headwinds and missteps, you still have a valuable hard asset, and one that increases in value in the long run due to inflation (chapter 15).

Too large can also be a problem, as mentioned by Swensen. He cautioned investing with very large sponsors, who generated such large fees just from management that they didn't need success and often lacked the hunger and drive to go after and maximize the best opportunities.[74]

TEAM DEPTH

Related to size is the sponsor's team depth. You want to see a diversified team with well-rounded skills, including these areas:

Underwriting. You want a team that knows how to build pro formas, identify and quantify the risks, evaluate markets, project exits, run stress tests, and build in contingencies.

Asset Management. You want someone on the team who is focused on asset management, carefully watching and measuring the performance of the investments to make sure they're performing as expected. And if they're not, a team that is able to troubleshoot and bring the resources to bear to solve the problem.

Back Office. You want a team that has systems and processes in place: accounting, back-office reporting expertise.

Experience. Although it might be fairly obvious, it's important to state that experience matters. Your operators should have experience in the asset classes in which they're investing. Pay attention as well to the size of the assets. For example, managing a 20-unit multifamily complex is different than managing a 200-unit complex.

TRANSPARENCY

Transparency is a subjective measurement but a very important one. You want operators who tell you the challenges and the problems, not just the victories. Ask your operator about the toughest challenge they have faced in business and how they handled it. Ask about their current challenges, and what "keeps them up" at night. You want to hear a transparent answer.

You want operators who readily share financials. It's always surprising to me to see operators who withhold financial information—that's a significant red flag. Anyone who is reticent to share financial information is hiding something. One great way to get a sense of an operator's transparency is to review their periodic investor updates from past projects. More illuminating still, ask for the investor updates on any projects that were struggling. Seeing how they actually handled these communications in the past can give you a good sense of how they may communicate challenges in the future.

As we have said, your adherence to the principles laid out in these last two chapters will be the most important factors determining your success as an alts investor: *allocation strategy* and *operator selection*. You will not be perfect as an investor, but perfection is not needed—discipline is enough. Resolve to be disciplined in these two areas.

So now we know something about selecting operators, but how do you avoid the losers altogether?

CHAPTER 17

HOW TO SPOT THE LOSERS

*"I think the biggest mistake is... trying to get rich quick.
It's pretty easy to get well-to-do slowly.
But it's not easy to get rich quick."*
- **Warren Buffet**

The number one reason investors avoid private alternatives is because they fear selecting a bad investment and losing everything. But I'll show you exactly how to spot the red flags that are common to the losers. First, let's hit the greatest fear of all, Ponzi schemes.

HOW TO SPOT A PONZI SCHEME

I personally invested in a Ponzi scheme in my early years. And I had friends who invested in two others.

Ponzi schemes are fraudulent businesses that use cash inflows from new investors to pay off previous investors. As long as they have more new investors putting cash in than existing investors getting paid off, they maintain the illusion of success. As soon as new investment inflows slow, they collapse.

Often Ponzi schemes do not start as fraudulent enterprises but as legitimate investments. But when they encounter disappointing results, they succumb to the temptation of fudging the numbers "temporarily" and start using new investors' capital to generate fake returns. Once they start down this path, things generally snowball, and it becomes impossible to recover.

However, investors' fears of them are quite overblown—you should know that Ponzi schemes are actually quite rare. There are about sixty Ponzi schemes discovered every year.[75] In the universe of twenty million LLCs in the US, that is a very small number. Most sponsors are honest, of course—it's extremely rare to find an investment business that's intentionally fraudulent.

They are also not difficult to spot. Here are some telltale ways to spot them.

High Returns. Every Ponzi scheme uses the promise of exceptionally high returns to lure new investors and convince them to ignore the warning signs. You might see investment returns quoted on a monthly or even weekly basis. For example, a currency trading scam promised 10–15 percent monthly returns. Never mind that at this rate of return, in a matter of ten years, a $1 investment would be worth trillions. Or the fact that if these returns were real, they wouldn't need your investment dollars.

Lots of Cash Flow. Most Ponzi schemes will return cash to your account quickly. The one I was involved in sent cash deposits of 50 to 75 percent profits after a three- to four-month investment period. This works to get investors both confident and exuberant and convince them to invite their friends and family to invest.

Secretive. Every Ponzi scheme I have ever looked at had a "secret sauce" that they protected. One had a carbon-capture technology they couldn't talk about because "big oil companies were trying to steal it." Another, a currency trading scam, would never share how they actually did it. Having some secret sauce, or a genius story, or a special "insider," convinces investors that the Ponzi scheme operators have something the rest of the world doesn't.

Unaudited. Almost without exception, Ponzi schemes are not audited by accounting firms. Auditors would quickly uncover the problem. Some may argue that Bernie Madoff's Ponzi scheme was audited, but it was audited by a captive firm with one client. Keep in mind that the absence of an audit does not mean something is amiss. Audits are expensive and painful for the operator, and typically only larger funds obtain them.

No Financials. Books and records are difficult to convincingly falsify, so most Ponzi schemes simply refuse to provide them, claiming secrecy or proprietary information.

Unqualified Frontmen. Every Ponzi scheme I have seen was represented by someone who engendered trust but was ultimately unqualified. In every case, they were completely clueless that they were representing a Ponzi scheme, and thus were utterly authentic, believable, and convincing because they themselves were convinced. The two trading scams were represented by beloved church pastors. The carbon capture scheme was represented by a businessman with no experience in energy technology.

TOO GOOD TO BE TRUE

The old adage—"If it sounds too good to be true, it probably is"—is absolutely correct. If you see annual returns above the 15–20 percent range, you should be alerted. Remember our discussion of compounding in chapter 4? Let's look at the profits generated by a $100,000 investment over twenty years at some higher rates of return:

Profits from $100,000 Compounded Monthly after 20 Years	
Annual Rate of Return	**Profits**
20%	$5 million
30%	$37 million
40%	$262 million
50%	$1.8 billion
100%	$22 trillion

You can see how quickly it becomes unrealistic. If these returns are truly attainable, then why do they need your investment money?

One of the currency trading scams I saw set up a very elaborate and convincing ruse. They used a legitimate third-party currency trading platform that allowed traders to set up unlimited free "paper-trading" accounts and program them with automated trading algorithms. The scammers would set up hundreds of accounts, each with a slightly different algorithm. They would run them all for several months, and inevitably a handful of them, by sheer happenstance, would demonstrate extraordinary returns. They would then demonstrate their top performer to prospective investors who could see and verify the historical paper trades were "real." Of course, the scammers never showed them the hundreds of other accounts that failed.

Most scams promise extraordinary returns that play on the innate greed in the human heart. Don't be fooled.

Not every high-yielding investment is a scam, of course. Recently my firm Aspen Funds offered an oil and gas investment with projections of 20–25 percent annual returns over ten years. We could offer these returns because of the extraordinarily low price at which we acquired the oil fields, reflecting the extremely negative market sentiment toward energy investments at that time. So far, it is playing out as projected.

We also offered distressed mortgage note investments in the aftermath of the Great Financial Crisis, and we projected and achieved high-teens returns for almost a decade.

Both of these funds were timed to take advantage of extreme but temporary market dislocations, and outsized returns can be generated in such circumstances—but only over limited periods of time.

OVER-LEVERAGE

Not every loser is a scam. Most, in fact, are just poorly conceived. The first category is over-leveraged investments. As we mentioned in chapter

2, there are two things that must be in place for smart debt. First, you must make sure the debt service can always be paid no matter what. Second, you must ensure that in a liquidation scenario you can recover your investment.

Leverage is an amplifier—it amplifies both returns and risk. Too much leverage, you add too much risk. Too little leverage, returns are too low. You are looking for the "Goldilocks zone"—not too hot and not too cold."

So how do you know the "just right" amount of debt? There are two tests.

The Income Test. When investment debt goes bad, it is less often about the *value* of the asset dropping, and more often about the *income* from the asset dropping. This is because as long as the debt is being paid, generally there is no issue with the debt. *Value* concerns do come into play but are usually less critical.

So when analyzing investments for risk levels, first measure the variance of income to make sure it can make its debt payments in a worst-case scenario. For example, apartment complexes are considered fairly safe, because people always need a place to live. Looking back through the worst years—the Great Recession, the COVID crisis, and the multifamily minibubble—we saw multi-family revenues drop in some areas by 10–20 percent. Properties financed with variable rate debt when interest rates melted up in 2022 caused properties to be unable to cover their debt payments.

Oil and gas investments are generally considered riskier, because the income can vary widely based on commodity prices. In 2016, the oil price crashed to $15, and in 2020, it crashed again to below zero.

So the level of leverage should correlate to the level of income risk. If income falls as much as it did in any of the worst years, can you still pay the debt?

Following this logic, you probably do not want to invest in a good multifamily deal with more than 70–75 percent leverage. Or an oil and gas investment with more than 20 percent leverage, unless they are hedging to protect against falling oil prices.

The Value Test. The second debt measure is *value*. This comes into play when the debt matures, or if the loan contains valuation covenants, or in cases where liquidation is forced, perhaps because of investor requirements. Use the same methodology as the income test: Look at price volatility during the worst years of the past, then add a cushion.

We'll show you how to analyze these things in chapter 19 "Decoding the Numbers."

Bubble Economics. During the multifamily mini bubble of 2020–2022, we saw many deals that were far too leveraged. Sponsors grossly overpaid for properties, purchasing deals at a 4 percent cap rate, which means a cash-on-cash return of just 4 percent. And because they were undercapitalized, they used 80 percent bridge debt and added 10 percent preferred equity to purchase the property, so investors were only supplying 10 percent of the capital as equity. This is extremely risky. If the market had more than a 10 percent correction, equity investors would be underwater.

In addition, the bridge debt had variable interest rates, with interest-only payments, and a three-year maturity. Thus, the property would no longer have positive cash flow if interest rates went up three years later—which in fact they did. Such an investment is a proverbial "bug looking for a windshield" and only works if everything goes exactly right. This is why you want to make sure you understand the cap table in every deal you invest in in real estate. Again, we'll cover all this in chapter 19.

AGGRESSIVE ASSUMPTIONS

Another fatal flaw is most often seen in younger, smaller sponsors: aggressive assumptions. For example, here are some things we have often seen:

- Assuming rents will rise by 10 percent per year because they did so last year.
- Assuming exit cap rates will be lower than acquisition cap rates.

- Assuming the property will achieve rents higher than market rents.
- Assuming you can rapidly raise rents without raising vacancy.
- Assuming aggressive lease-up rates.
- Assuming interest rates will drop.
- Assuming little need for cash reserves.
- Assuming aggressive development time frames.

You get the idea. My goal here is not to list every possible ridiculous assumption, but to show how easily a sponsor can juice the numbers. By just adding an inflation escalation of more than 2 percent or dropping the exit cap rate by 1.5 percent, I can make the worst investment imaginable show incredible returns.

That's why it's so important to choose sponsors you trust to underwrite conservatively and to study the pro forma yourself. We'll show you how in chapter 19.

FEE GENERATORS

Every private investment includes fees for the sponsor. Fees are how the sponsor covers their costs and expects to profit from their effort and skill in operating the investment. You want the sponsors to be properly incentivized to maximize your investment. But you also want them to care more about you as an investor than the fees they generate from you.

As I mentioned in chapter 16 in the co-investment section, many investments are structured more as fee generators for the sponsor than as good investments for investors. It is critical you learn to spot them. It's not that difficult. Everything you need to know to identify fee-generator deals can be found in the PPM (we'll cover fees in more detail in chapter 18 "Navigate a PPM In 30 Minutes").

The Fee Spectrum

Modest Fees
High sponsor co-investment
Strong alignment of interest
Higher returns
Investor-First

High Fees
Low sponsor co-investment
Poor alignment of interest
Lower returns
Sponsor-First

Here's how you can spot the "sponsor first" fee-generator deals. They have high fees, especially sales fees, up-front fees, and management fees. Here are the fees you should pay special attention to in order of concern:

Sales Fees (Placement Fees). Sales fees are commissions paid to broker-dealers for selling you the investment. Broker-dealers are licensed entities that are legally allowed to take commissions from raising investment capital. As an investor, you need to realize that broker-dealers are salesmen incentivized to sell you the investment. I generally am not too worried about sales fees below the 2 percent range. But I have seen sales fees as high as 10 percent. This is a telltale sign that an investment is designed as a fee generator.

In David Swensen's book *Unconventional Success*, he gives a scathing example of a fee generator: the Wells Private REIT.[76] Before acquiring a single asset, it carried hefty fees—broker-dealer commissions of 7 percent, dealer manager fees (whatever that is) of 2.5 percent, organization and offering expenses of 3 percent. To acquire properties, they added 3 percent acquisition fees, plus 0.5 percent for expenses. After purchasing properties, they charged leasing fees of 4.5 percent of gross revenues.

If they sold properties, they collected 3 percent of the sales price, and then 10 percent of the profits generated. If that wasn't enough, they also charged 2 percent for employee stock options.

As mentioned, fees are normal and necessary—but fees should be commensurate with value added, effort expended, and costs incurred. In the case of Wells, they focused on purchasing new, high-grade office and industrial buildings with triple-net leases—hardly high value-add, high-effort, or high-cost.

Other Upfront Fees. Also look at other up-front fees like acquisition fees. I usually don't mind acquisition fees in the range of 1–3 percent if the fees are commensurate with the effort required to acquire the assets.

> **FEE GENERATOR DEALS HAVE HIGH FEES, ESPECIALLY IN SALES FEES, OTHER UP-FRONT FEES, AND MANAGEMENT FEES.**

Management Fees. The next red flag is high management fees (usually charged monthly or quarterly). I usually am not concerned with fees in the 0.5–1 percent range annually, and I am open to 2 percent fees if high management effort is required.

Performance Fees. The least concerning are performance fees (fees paid on the resulting profits).

David Swensen was very focused on sponsor fees. He thought fees could align interests with investors or misalign interests. Ideally, he wanted management fees to just cover their operating costs, and have the bulk of their compensation come from performance fees.

Don't reject all high-fee investments out of hand—especially higher performance fees. My own firm, Aspen Funds, charged performance fees of 50 percent of profits on our early distressed debt funds. However, we had an enormous cost structure related to resolving the debt. Rather than charging our costs directly to investors, we took the risk and absorbed the costs, paying for them out of our fees on profits.

I had my own experience with a fee generator. CrowdStreet is a popular real estate investment portal, and in 2023, the *Wall Street Journal* published an expose of their unscrupulous behavior. I invested with them in the redevelopment of the Union Station in Salt Lake City into a Marriott Hotel. They originally raised capital for a $55 million construction build. Just months later, I received a letter saying that the cost would actually be $80 million, 45 percent higher than expected. Any decent developer obtains a G-Max (guaranteed maximum price) construction agreement prior to raising capital, but apparently not these sponsors.

They went back to existing investors for a capital call (a request for more capital). But it was now a significantly worse story.

Their senior lender dropped out, and the junior lender stepped up, but at a floating interest rate of SOFR+760 (7.85 percent at a time when fixed rates were around 5 percent). The last time I checked, they were paying 12.9 percent for their senior loan.

Not surprisingly, even though construction and interest costs skyrocketed, the sponsor provided a new pro forma showing higher projected revenues than originally provided. Somehow this project "magically" was going to achieve the same high returns as the original pro forma.

CrowdStreet offered this capital call to existing investors, and it predictably failed.

CrowdStreet then went out to raise money from new investors with a new offering, in which I was unable to find any disclosure of the material facts:

- The new raise was the result of a failed capital call.
- The senior lender had bailed.
- The new lender's rates were incredibly high and variable.
- The developer blew out their budget by $25M (45 percent) and failed to obtain a G-Max contract.

CrowdStreet successfully completed the raise—and made additional fees from it! They are a licensed broker-dealer, which means they are legally allowed to take commissions from raising investment capital, regardless of how good the deal is or how well it performs. Anytime you see a broker-dealer offering a deal, you should ask a few more questions.

> **HIGH SPONSOR CO-INVESTMENT IS THE #1 WAY TO ENSURE AGAINST FEE GENERATOR DEALS.**

Co-Investment. I mentioned the importance of co-investment in chapter 16 to identify good operators, but a lack of sponsor co-investment is also a quick-and-dirty way to spot fee generators. High sponsor co-investment is the number one way to ensure against fee-generator deals. Any sponsor designing an investment primarily to generate fees will not be interested in investing their own capital in their deals. And sponsors designing great investments will be eager to put their own capital to work.

> **MAKE SURE FUNDS ARE USED APPROPRIATELY, NOT TO FUND MANAGEMENT OPERATIONS OR BUY OUT EXISTING INVESTORS.**

Use of Funds. I have seen a land-development deal that charged fees of 80 percent of profits after paying investors a 20 percent hurdle rate. Even more shocking was the "Use of Funds," which allowed the sponsor to use investor capital to pay the operator's salaries and overhead expenses. There was no cap on expenses. Clearly, this is a "sponsor first" fee generator. Not surprisingly, the sponsor had no co-investment in the deal.

I saw another deal where funds were used to buy out management. So again, make sure funds are used appropriately, not to fund management operations or buy out existing investors.

But even if you can select a sponsor, can a normal person understand the intimidating subscription documents that accompany private alts? Next, I'll show you how to break down a PPM in about thirty minutes.

CHAPTER 18

NAVIGATE A PPM IN THIRTY MINUTES

"A lawyer is a person who writes a 10,000-word document and calls it a 'brief.'"
- **Franz Kafka**

When you invest passively, you will almost always receive a private placement memorandum (PPM). This can be a one-hundred-plus-page legal document that is the official offering. It can feel daunting to read, but it is a *very* important document to understand.

The purpose of the PPM is to

1. Show you important legal disclosures.
2. Tell you what you need to know about the investment to make a good choice.
3. Protect the sponsor from investor lawsuits.

I can tell you that most investors simply sign it with little more than a cursory reading, if at all. In this chapter, we want to show you how to confidently navigate a PPM and the things you should focus on.

First, don't be intimidated by the legal jargon. Even a novice can get through a PPM in a short time. Block out thirty minutes of focused time.

As you read, underline everything you don't understand. Build a list of questions and then call and talk to the sponsor. Don't ever move forward if you feel uncomfortable. A solid sponsor should have no problem walking through all your questions. If they don't, that is a red flag.

Now, let's look at the general structure or flow of a PPM; then we'll get into specific things to look for.

THE STRUCTURE OF A PPM

Notices. At the top of the PPM is usually a few pages of legal notices and disclosures. These originate from a myriad of federal and state laws that require specific notices and disclosures. You can skip this section.

Key Terms. This section will be very valuable to you as an investor. It's going to summarize all the key terms of the investment:
- Fees to the sponsor.
- Minimum investment amounts.
- Distributions. How they plan on distributing profits.
- Duration. How long they expect to be in the investment.
- Redemption and liquidity options (if any).
- Manager removal. Your rights to remove the manager.
- Reporting. What you should expect regarding reports.
- Expenses. What expenses the sponsor is allowed to charge the fund.
- Managers, administrators, auditors, your rights (or lack thereof).
- Any other terms that affect your investment.

Business Plan. This section is going to tell you exactly what the sponsor plans on doing to make money in the investment. You should absolutely make sure you understand (and like!) what they plan on doing with your funds. As long as the sponsor adheres to this business plan, they have reasonable assurance of steering clear of liability to investors for poor performance.

Risk Factors. This will be one of the largest sections. Sponsors and lawyers want to put every possible thing that could go wrong, regardless of how remote. In this section, they will tell you all the reasons why you *shouldn't* invest. The idea is that if they warn you of the risks, any problems they encounter are on you, the investor.

This section is the most challenging to get through, because it is a mixture of lawyer's boilerplate and real risks you need to think about. Boilerplate items include things like "government regulations might change," "we have little operating history," and "our founders might die."

> **Experienced investors pay more attention to the risks than the upside potential.**

Real risks might include things like high debt loads, variable interest rates, development or construction risks, and budget and timeline risks.

As you go through this section, highlight the risks you want to learn more about, or think about further.

Remembering all the way back to chapter 1, in the game of investing, protecting against losses is far more important than maximizing gains. To be a successful investor in alts, you must take only prudent risks. In assessing deals, *experienced investors pay more attention to the risks than the upside potential*.

Operating Agreement. The operating agreement is the legal governing document of the investment company. It includes every important matter regarding how the investment company will run. Generally, the Key Terms section of the PPM summarizes everything you need to know about the Operating Agreement, so you can skip or scan this section unless you want the nitty-gritty details.

Tax. This section usually contains very complicated language regarding how tax allocations will be made. Most investments will allocate taxes pro rata with distributions made, or, if there has been none, pro rata with investment amount. Read this section to see if that's what they are doing. If you can't understand it, mark it and ask the sponsor to explain how they plan on making tax allocations, or give it to your CPA to explain to you.

ERISA. This section pertains to benefit plan investors. You can safely skip it. ERISA is the Employee Retirement Income Security Act, and if the operator accepts more than 25 percent of its funds from retirement benefit plans, it is subject to a host of very challenging regulations and fiduciary obligations. This section details why the investment may not be suitable for benefits plans. If you are investing your IRA funds, technically you are a benefit plan, but you shouldn't trigger the 25 percent rule.

Regulatory. This section contains details regarding regulatory items pertaining to the fund. Scan this section to understand regulatory concerns.

THE BUSINESS PLAN

Again, the business plan is how they plan on using your investment capital to make money, how they plan to allocate the funds, the timelines they expect to complete the plan, and how they ultimately expect to realize the value created (i.e., disposition).

You want to read this section fully and comprehend it. If there are things you don't understand, you should call the sponsor and go through it until you do. If, after the call, you still don't understand, you should probably pass on the investment.

You may not be an expert in their business, but do not discount your gut! How realistic does this seem? What are the key assumptions they are making in their investment thesis? What are the key risks? How are they managing the risks? How experienced is the team? These are all things that you can answer at an intuitive level.

Key Things to Look For: Fees

First and foremost among the things you want to grasp are sponsor fees. As noted earlier, sponsor fees can make or break a deal.

Not all fees are equal—some align your interests, and some create a divergence of interests. You want to clearly understand all the fees and how they align your interests or not. Here are the fees that might be part of your deal.

Sales (Placement) Fees. These are sales commissions paid to a licensed broker-dealer for convincing you to invest. Broker-dealers are generally *not* on the sponsor team, and typically have no other stake in the deal. So once they have sold you the investment, they receive their fee and will no longer be involved. They are not fiduciaries, meaning they have little obligation to you, the investor. Sales fees create misalignment of interests. I have seen placement fees anywhere from 2 percent to 10 percent. I personally wouldn't consider investing in anything above 2 percent. Many institutions will not pay any sales fees at all.

Acquisition (or Origination) Fees. These are fees paid to the sponsor related to the purchase of investment assets. It can be very time-consuming and expensive to find, evaluate, negotiate, and close investments. These fees help the sponsor cover those costs. You want them to be high enough to make sure the sponsor's efforts are covered, but not so high that the sponsor wants to close as many deals as possible regardless of quality. I typically wouldn't balk at acquisition fees in the 1–3 percent range as long as they are justified by the effort required. Anything beyond that should be questioned.

Management (or AUM) Fees. These are ongoing fees charged at regular intervals (annually, quarterly, or monthly) to cover the sponsor's overhead, asset management, accounting, and reporting efforts. You want your sponsors to be able to keep their doors open, have regular calls with property managers, continually analyze operating and risk metrics, monitor the performance of the investments, and bring to bear any extra effort necessary when the investment encounters challenges. This all takes effort and staff.

You want the fees high enough that the sponsor can afford to manage the investments, but not so high they care more about collecting their management fees than about the performance of the investment. I don't mind fees in the 0.5–2 percent annual range as long as they are justified by effort. Beware of paying fees at the higher end of this range if there is not much management required. Also, ensure that these fees are tied to some level of performance of the underlying asset. As an example, in real estate, AUM fees are normally calculated as a percentage of effective gross income (EGI). This way if the performance of the property suffers, the sponsor is incentivized to improve it.

Disposition (or Exit Fees). These fees are paid when an asset is sold. Like acquisition fees, there can be significant effort in finding buyers, and negotiating and closing the sale. However, I don't generally like this fee—it should be modest or zero. Since the disposition of an investment should generate profits, which they are sharing, why do they need this fee? You want them to be more incentivized to maximize your profits, not just close a sale.

Profits Fees (aka Performance, Income, Carried Interest, or Promote Fees). These are the profit-sharing fees. You want this to be the most significant fee collected by your sponsor. Why? Because they get paid when you do, and the more money you make, the more they make. These fees come the closest to aligning your interests with your sponsor.

Pay attention to the proportion of these fees relative to all others. Too small, and your sponsor is going to be happy to sit back and passively collect maintenance fees rather than make sure the investment performs well. Too large, and your sponsor is incentivized to take extraordinary risk because of their big upside. Both *too low* and *too high* profits fees can create extra risk for you. These risks can be minimized by high co-investment from your sponsor.

Other (potential hidden) Fees. Over the years, I have seen a variety of other fees that sponsors may charge. Examples include loan guarantor fees, development fees, construction management fees, refinance fees, loan servicing fees, etc. While any of these fees can be justified, it is important to step back and ask yourself if the fee fits the business plan. Also, when sponsors start to add many layers of fees to an investment, that reduces profit margin and can create misalignment of interests.

Red Flags. Here are some areas that should be red flags for investors. Not every red flag should be an automatic pass, but simply discussion points with the sponsor—there may be legitimate dynamics in play. In the end, it's important to ask yourself, *What is this fee incentivizing?*

Here are some common red flags to look for in fees:

- Any sales (placement) fees
- High or unjustified acquisition fees
- High or unjustified management fees
- High or unjustified disposition fees
- Low proportion of profits fees relative to other fees
- High proportion of profits fees relative to other fees

Expenses

Expenses is another section that bears scrutiny. Some expenses are benign and sensible, and others are not. Most offerings I have seen have no extraordinary expense provisions, but you should make sure there are no surprises. Here are some expenses you might encounter.

Operational Expenses. These should be only direct, hard costs incurred by the investment—things like financing costs, transaction fees, property management, professional fees, insurance expenses, legal and litigation-related, indemnification expenses, taxes, etc.

Organizational Expenses. These are typically costs incurred for the formation of the entity, things like legal expenses, licenses, filing fees, etc.

Offering Expenses. These are sales-related expenses paid to the sponsor for selling investors. It can include things like travel, entertainment, marketing, and advertising. These expenses should *not* be allowed except in limited amounts. Do you want to pay your sponsor's investor sales and marketing costs? They should be covered out of the sponsor's fees.

Overhead (or General and Administrative). These are the sponsor's operating costs, things like salaries, rents, and office supplies. These should *not* be allowed. Such costs should be covered out of the sponsor's management fees.

Red Flags. Here's what you should look out for:

- Offering expenses. Why should you pay the sponsor's sales costs?
- Overhead. This is an automatic hard pass. An investor should *not* pay a sponsor's internal costs. Think about the misalignment created if you are paying for the sponsor's corporate retreats, luxurious offices, exorbitant salaries, etc.

The Waterfall

This concept catches a lot of first-time private investors off guard. But understanding the waterfall is both critical and not difficult to master. The waterfall describes exactly how income is allocated both in *priority* and *amount* or *split*. Here's an example.

1. **"First, income is used to pay expenses."** This makes sense; the investment must pay its vendors and costs before investors.
    In real estate, income would be rents collected, and expenses

would include things like utilities, maintenance, and the property manager.
2. **"Second, income will go to management fees."** This is also common to cover the sponsor's overhead.
3. **"Third, income will go to investor accruals."** Let's say the investment makes regular payments to investors. If there is a lag in initial cash flow or a shortfall down the road, this provision prioritizes catch-up payments.
4. **"Fourth, income will be allocated to the investor until they received a 6 percent return."** This is called the "hurdle rate" or "preferred return," because it is the minimum rate of return to the investor before the manager can get a profit share. This is common in real estate deals, but rarer in other investment classes.
5. **"Finally, remaining income will be split between the investor and the manager 80/20 percent."** This is the profit-sharing arrangement between the investor and the sponsor/manager.

Keep in mind that there might be multiple waterfalls—one for cash flow and another for dispositions. For example, a common arrangement has cash flow from operations (like real estate rent payments) go to investors 100 percent, but income from an exit (like the sale of a property) be split with the sponsor.

It is also common to have multiple share classes, each with its own waterfall. Our firm does this to accommodate different investor check sizes. For example, a $100,000 investor might get a 6 percent preferred return and a 70 percent profit split; an institutional investor with a $5 million check might get an 8 percent preferred return and a 90 percent profit split.

Red Flags. Waterfall warnings include:

- Where sponsor fees are prioritized above investors. As mentioned above, it is common for a modest management fee to be prioritized, but the bulk of the sponsor's compensation should be based on *performance*, and the sponsor should be *last* in line, after investors are paid.
- If there is no hurdle rate (see above). A hurdle rate makes sure you get paid a reasonable return before the sponsor starts taking their cut of profits.
- Where the sponsor gets the majority of the profit split—e.g., 80 percent to the sponsor and 20 percent to the investor. We've seen this many times and again, it creates a mismatched alignment.
- If the waterfall seems very complicated and includes provisions such as a GP catch-up prior to a profit split.
- If what is presented in the waterfall is different from what is presented in their investor pro forma.

Use of Funds

This can be difficult to find (if at all), but you should make an effort. It may be a separate section, or it may be embedded or implied in the business plan or expenses sections.

Red Flags. I have seen use of funds include:
- Retiring existing debt
- Compensating founders with bonuses or dividends
- Buying out other investors, sometimes at a premium
- Paying salaries and overhead
- Paying related parties lump sum payments
- Buying unnecessary buildings or equipment

Not all these red flags constitute a hard pass, but most should. You need to know exactly how the sponsor intends to spend your investment dollars and make sure it aligns with your expectations and sound business practices.

Distributions

The last important area to note concerns distributions. You might be confused here. Didn't we just cover this in the waterfall? The waterfall covers *income*, and distributions cover *cash payments to investors*. It is important to understand the distinction. An investment can have income but no distributions, and vice versa. Let me illustrate.

> You need to know exactly how the sponsor intends to spend your investment dollars.

Income can be earned by an investment with no cash to pay investors. Examples would include selling an asset at a profit, then using the proceeds to buy another. The sale generates income, but the purchase drains the cash available for distribution.

Distributions can also be made to investors without any income generated. For example, selling a property at cost and returning capital to investors, or a lender releasing funds held in reserve, or a cash-out refinance.

Most investments entail "distributable cash," which is cash left over after reserving funds for operational needs. This is usually very broad, giving the sponsor a lot of latitude to determine distributions. This is not a red flag.

Red Flags. The biggest caution here is *phantom income*. Phantom income happens in situations like the first example above where profits are earned, but distributions are not paid. In this case you will owe taxes on the earnings, but without distributions to pay them.

Talk to Your Sponsor

Most inexperienced investors will not ask a lot of questions of their sponsors for fear of looking inexperienced or asking a dumb question. But better to look like a fool than write a check for a poor investment that proves you one!

As a long-time sponsor, I can tell you we appreciate investors that take the time to understand their investment. And we are more than happy to take the time for investors who care to learn and understand, even if their check size is small.

And although I am a very experienced investor, I am still always learning, and I find myself asking "stupid" questions of sponsors all the time—shamelessly, I might add! If you don't ask, you will never learn, and that's the only thing that would truly make you "stupid." If you find your sponsor impatient or condescending, you should probably find another sponsor.

Do this: Make the call to your sponsor and ask the questions!

So you've navigated a PPM, but what about the numbers? Can you get your head around that? Trust me, you can, and it's worth the effort. Now it's time to decode them.

CHAPTER 19

DECODING THE NUMBERS

*"As long as algebra is taught in school,
there will be prayer in school."*
- **Cokie Roberts**

When I started my dot-com, I wrote a business plan to pitch my company to venture capitalists. But when I got to the finance plan section, I didn't know what to do. I didn't have any understanding of finances at all. I fiddled through it as best I could and stuck it at the back, hoping no one would pay attention to it. I would get so excited in my pitches, talking about my vision for the company, the incredible opportunity, etc. But without fail, before I could get to the really exciting stuff, these VCs would skip ahead right to the back of the book to the finance plan. I would always get a lump in my throat, feeling sunk.

Today, when I read business plans, the finance section is the first place I go after I understand the basics of the product or service. The finance plan tells me everything—the margins, growth plan, spending targets, cash flow, exit strategy, and more.

This will probably be the most daunting chapter for many folks. But take heart: If I could grasp it, you can too. And you don't have to become a finance expert. Even a most basic understanding will help you be successful and avoid mistakes.

THE IRR FALLACY

Before we jump in, it's worthwhile to understand *returns*—obviously, our main objective as investors.

Higher returns are always better, right? Not always! *Higher returns don't always make you more money.* Returns are far more nuanced than most realize. Let me illustrate with a few examples. First, consider a $100,000 in Investment A that pays out $200,000 in year five, like this:

IRR on $100,000 Investment A							
Year	1	2	3	4	5	IRR	ARR
Payout	0	0	0	0	200,000	14.9%	20.0%

The Average Annualized Return (AAR) is 20 percent—100 percent profit divided by the five years it took to earn it. But the Internal Rate of Return (IRR) is less, 14.9 percent. This is because IRR accounts for the *time value of money*. Another way to think about it is the IRR calculates *compounded* returns. A $100,000 investment compounded at 14.9 percent would be worth $200,000 after five years.

> **Higher returns don't always make you more money.**

Let's look at a different investment, B, which makes regular annual payments of $40,000 per year:

IRR on $100,000 Investment A								
Year	1	2	3	4	5	IRR	ARR
Payout	40,000	40,000	40,000	40,000	40,000	28.6%	20.0%

Notice the AAR is the same—we received $200,000, a profit of $100,000 over five years, same as investment A. But the IRR is way higher, 28.6 percent, because the cash was returned at a faster pace.

The textbooks will tell you IRR is a better measure of return, *but it can be quite misleading.* Let's look at two examples side by side, and you can see how a *lower IRR might actually make you more money.*

Investment A has a 14.9 percent IRR by paying a single lump sum of $200,000 after five years. Let's compare that to Investment C, which has a higher IRR, 15.2 percent. You should take the second, right? Here are the payment schedules:

IRR on $100,000 Investment A								
Year	1	2	3	4	5	IRR	ARR
Payout	0	0	0	0	200,000	14.9%	20.0%

IRR on $100,000 Investment C								
Year	1	2	3	4	5	IRR	ARR
Payout	0	100,000	0	0	50,000	15.2%	10.0%

Investment C returns 100 percent of your initial investment capital in year two, then another $50,000 in year five. Yes, the IRR is higher, but the total return is *lower*—you only made $50,000 in profits, half of Investment A.

So which investment should you make?

The answer depends on this: If you were to invest in C, *what would you do with the $100,000 you receive in year two?* If you have another opportunity ready and waiting to earn 15.2 percent or better, then yes, Investment

B is a better opportunity. But if you were to put it in cash—perhaps because you didn't know what else to do with it, or couldn't find something good—then Investment A is the better option.

IRR assumes 100 percent efficiency in your capital deployment, which is far from the case. Investments that return capital faster have higher IRRs but also require more effort from you to keep the funds deployed.

UNDERSTANDING THE CAPITAL STACK

Now let's dive into how to evaluate deals. The place to start is understanding the capital structure—or "stack"—which is how all the money in the investment is arranged. This is very important. After operator selection, the capital stack is the primary factor that determines your risk. We will use real estate examples, but it applies to all deals. Here are the basic categories:

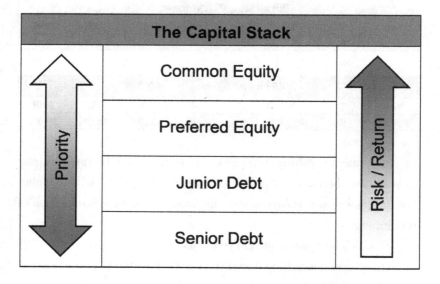

Figure 60: The Capital Stack

Senior Debt. We'll again use our $10 million apartment complex to illustrate. Senior debt is the loan typically from a bank or other lender. They will require monthly payments and usually have performance covenants like certain levels of cash flow. They will have liens on the assets, enabling them to collect through foreclosure. They have the highest priority—meaning they are the first money out and will get paid everything owed before anyone else gets a dime. Investing in senior debt carries the least risk and yields the lowest returns.

Junior Debt. Sometimes called second liens, subordinated debt, mezzanine or mezz debt, this is next in priority. They are next to get paid after the senior debt is satisfied. Junior debt may or may not be present, and there may also be multiple junior lenders, each successively lower in priority. They may also have liens on the assets, and thus can also initiate foreclosure.

Preferred Equity. This is a blend between debt and equity and is generally less common. Preferred equity is typically from large institutions and can be quite complex, with all or few of the following provisions.

- Control rights. They may have the right to take over the deal or force a sale.
- Performance covenants. They may have requirements like maintaining certain levels of cash flow or valuation.
- Payments. They typically have monthly cash payment requirements as well as additional payments that accrue.
- Participation. They may also get paid a percentage of the profits out of cash flow or exit.

> Even when deals completely fail, it is common for investors lower in the capital stack to do well and even profit.

Common Equity. This is last in priority. They start getting paid only after everyone else is fully paid. But they also receive any remaining profits.

Thus, when a deal works very well, common equity is typically the biggest winner. And when a deal doesn't work well, common equity is the biggest loser. Even when deals completely fail, it is common for investors lower in the capital stack to do well and even profit.

Map Out the "Cap Table"

The "cap table" is the table that shows the capital stack. It is wise to draw the cap table for a potential deal. Put percentages for each category as well as the key terms for each.

For example, let's lay out the cap table for an equity investment in a value-add apartment complex deal with a five-year business plan and projected 25 percent returns for common equity investors. Start at the bottom:

What do you notice about this cap table? Here are a few observations you should pick up on.

1. The leverage is very high—90 percent (add up everything below common equity). That alone makes this deal *very* risky.
2. A variable rate senior debt means there is a significant interest rate risk here, and you need to consider what may happen to the deal if rates go up.
3. The junior debt matures in three years. But if the business plan calls for a five-year exit, what are they going to do to pay this loan off in three years? If they can't refinance, they will default.
4. The preferred equity gets 12 percent returns before common equity gets anything, and they also take 5 percent of profits. That's very rich, and they are ahead of you!

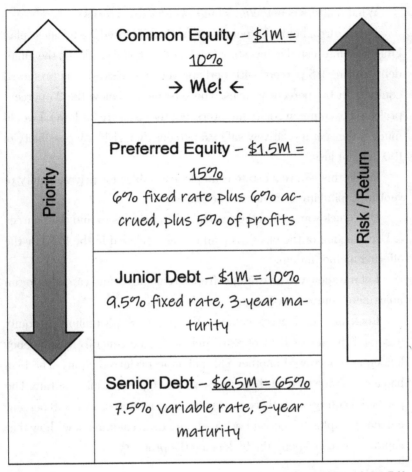

Figure 61: Example Cap Table

Even if I absolutely loved this asset and business plan, I would pass on this deal. Many unsophisticated investors would be enticed by the high headline returns. But this example clearly illustrates that even if I thought those returns were possible, the risk is too high. The reason the returns are likely so high is directly related to the deal's high leverage. Leverage is an amplifier—the more you have, the higher the projected returns.

What matters is not *returns* but *risk-adjusted* returns.

Let me drive home this point even further. If I loved the business plan, I might be interested in investing lower in the capital stack—in the junior debt earning 9.5 percent with perhaps very low risk, or the preferred equity with 12+ percent returns. The returns are below the 25 percent projected to common equity investors, but the risks are far lower. I would much rather get a relatively safe 9.5 percent than risk any possibility of 100 percent loss.

While this is a real estate example, cap tables for private equity or venture capital investments will be similar.

One quick way to find the "cap table" in a deal is to find the Sources & Uses section of the business plan usually included in the PPM or the offering memorandum.

Let me show you an example from a real budget and cap table for an apartment complex we bought:

Look at the Sources column. We put in $14.5 million in equity, assumed the senior debt of $23.3 million (46 percent) from an agency lender, and borrowed another $12 million in preferred equity. The loan had a remaining term of three years with a 3.9 percent interest rate. The preferred equity had a three-year term and an interest rate of 8 percent current pay, plus 6.5 percent accrued. The Uses column shows how that capital was to be spent, the bulk being the property.

The Pro Forma

Next, find the pro forma. This is usually a table or spreadsheet provided by the sponsor.

The pro forma shows income over time. It can be by year, quarter, or month. For each time period, it will show revenues, expenses, and net profits. This table—or another like it—will also show capital events, like property improvement expenditures, refinance events, and sale. And it

Sources		Uses	
Senior Debt	23,240,000	Purchase	44,340,000
Preferred Equity	12,000,000	Closing Costs	665,100
Equity	14,564,161	Capex	2,333,205
		CM Fee	186,656
		Working Capital	200,000
		Interest Reserves	600,000
		Financing costs	232,400
		Acquisition Fee	886,800
		Upfront Pref Eq fee	300,000
		Pref Broker	60,000
Total	49,804,161		49,804,161

Figure 62: The Louis Apartments Cap Table

will show your calculated returns. Here is an example from the same apartment complex:

Cash Flow Summary	1	2	3	4	5
Inflation Rate			3%	3%	3%
Total Potential Rent	5,027,520	5,178,346	5,333,696	5,493,707	5,658,518
Other Income	420,542	433,159	446,153	459,538	473,324
Total Potential Income	5,448,062	5,611,504	5,779,849	5,953,245	6,131,842
Vacancy, Bad debt, LTL	(1,555,422)	(984,819)	(378,580)	(389,938)	(401,636)
Effective Gross Income	3,892,641	4,626,685	5,401,269	5,563,307	5,730,207
Opex	1,593,286	1,641,085	1,690,317	1,741,027	1,793,257
Property Management	116,779	138,801	162,038	166,899	171,906
Replacement Reserves	50,000	51,500	53,045	54,636	56,275
Total Operating Ex.	1,760,065	1,831,385	1,905,400	1,962,562	2,021,439
NOI	2,132,575	2,795,300	3,495,869	3,600,745	3,708,768
Asset Mgmt Fees	116,779	138,801	162,038	166,899	171,906
Debt Service	1,315,388	1,315,388	1,315,388	2,272,315	2,272,315
DSCR	1.62x	2.13x	2.66x	1.32x	1.36x
Before Tax Cash Flow	700,408	1,341,111	2,018,443	1,161,531	1,264,546
Net Refi Proceeds	-	-	15,772,117	-	-
Net Sale Proceeds	-	-	-	-	31,005,196
Total Cash Flow & Sale	700,408	1,341,111	17,790,560	1,161,531	32,269,742

Figure 63: The Louis Apartments Cash Flow

Let me walk you through it.

Across the top is each year.

Total Potential Rent (also called gross potential rent) is the rental income if every unit were 100 percent rented at the target rental rates.

Other Income is things like late fees, utility bill backs, pet fee income, etc.

Total Potential Income is the total of those two items.

Vacancy, Bad Debt, LTL (Loss to Lease) is the amount of income lost due to vacancy, collections, discounts, and rental rates below target rents; for example, from legacy leases below targeted rates. This is usually a negative number reducing the GPR.

Effective Gross Income (EGI) is the sum of all that, the total income.

OpEx is the operating expenses, like utilities, maintenance, property taxes, insurance, etc.

Property Management is the fee paid to the property management company.

Replacement Reserves is the amount reserved for ongoing unit turnover.

Net Operating Income (NOI) is the total of all the above: the income of the property excluding debt service and sponsor fees. This is an important number—NOI determines the value of the property. The value of the property is NOI divided by cap rate.

Asset Management Fees are taken by the sponsor to manage the asset.

Debt Service is the payment made to the lender.

Debt Service Coverage Ratio (DSCR) is the ratio of NOI to debt payments. This is a very important number to banks—they like to see 1.25x or better.

Net Refi Proceeds are the proceeds realized from a refinance after paying off the lender.

Net Sale Proceeds are the proceeds realized from a sale after paying off the lender.

As you can see, we projected positive cash flow throughout, a refinance in year three that would generate $15.7 million in net proceeds, and a sale in year five that would generate $31 million in net proceeds on our $14.5 million investment.

Cap Rates. Before we move on, we should explain cap rates. The *cap rate* is the main valuation metric used by real estate investors. The cap rate for a property is the net operating earnings (NOI) divided by the value of the property. So, it is the *unlevered yield* of the property—the yield of the property if you paid cash. You can compare it to a bond.

Cap rates vary by property type, location, and age, and—like interest rates—they change over time with the macroeconomic environment.

For bonds, the price and the yield have an inverse relationship—if the yield drops, the value of the bond rises, and vice versa. Real estate is the same—if the cap rate drops, the value of the property rises, and vice versa.

Simple algebra tells us that the value of a property is NOI divided by the cap rate. So, a property with $1 million in NOI, at a 5 percent cap rate, would be worth $20 million. If cap rates rise to 6.5 percent, the value would drop to $15.4 million.

> **Return projections are simply the result of a spreadsheet exercise requiring a lot of guesses.**

Assumptions

What inexperienced investors may not realize is that return projections are simply the result of a spreadsheet exercise *requiring a lot of guesses*. We make our best guesses and call them *assumptions*. Assumptions include things like:
- Future interest rates
- Future growth rates
- Future inflation rates

- Future demand
- Future valuation metrics (cap rates)

As you might imagine, different assumptions can wildly change the outcomes! Some assumptions are especially sensitive. For example:
- Simply changing our annual inflation rate (or annual rate of rent increases) assumption from 3 percent to 5 percent boosts our expected cash flow by 10 percent and our exit profits by 13 percent. That is a seemingly small change but has a disproportionate impact on projected returns.
- Changing our sale cap rate from 5.25 percent to 4.25 percent boosted our sale profits by 70 percent. This is another highly sensitive variable and often has the largest impact of total return. Because the sponsor can't control this (market-driven) number, it is important to stress-test to understand the range of outcomes. Sponsors often increase cap rate at exit to not be overly aggressive. However, if they are showing a lower cap rate at exit, that's a yellow flag, or at least requires a justifiable reason.

You can see how easy it would be for sponsors to "juice" their projected returns—which is another reason you should never base your investment decision on headline returns.

You can learn a lot about the sponsors by looking at their assumptions! Among the crazy things we have seen:
- 10 percent per year projected rent growth from inflation
- A Bitcoin fund projecting the price of rising from $40,000 to $325,000 within two years
- A tech company going from one to one hundred employees in its first year (can you say "chaos"?)

Back to our example: Based on about $14,100 per unit for renovations of older units and roughly $1 million in upgraded exteriors and amenities, we projected we could increase rents by 31 percent. The "T12" column show trailing twelve-month rents for the various unit types as purchased, and the "Pro forma" column shows our target rents. "R" units are already renovated units. **T12 Rent/SF** shows existing rents averaged $1.13 per square foot, and our pro forma target rents, **PF Rent/SF**:

Unit Mix / Rents and Rent Targets						
Type	**# Units**	**T12**	**Proforma**	**Sq Ft**	**T12 Rent/SF**	**PF Rent/SF**
2x2 flat	3	$1,112	$1,725	1,036	$1.07	$1.67
2x2 flat R	1	$1,353	$1,650	1,036	$1.31	$1.59
2x2 th	34	$1,344	$1,975	1,208	$1.11	$1.63
2x2 th R	52	$1,535	$1,850	1,208	$1.27	$1.53
3x2 flat	3	$1,480	$1,995	1,296	$1.14	$1.54
3x2 flat R	1	$1,840	$1,950	1,296	$1.42	$1.50
3x2.5 th	47	$1,584	$2,300	1,612	$0.98	$1.43
3x2.5 th R	59	$1,820	$2,250	1,612	$1.13	$1.40
			Weighted Average:		**$1.13**	**$1.49**

Figure 64: The Louis Apartments Historical and Targets Rents

That is a big increase in rent. How did we know this was achievable? We looked up rents for nearby properties of similar vintage and amenities. The table below shows they are in line with the market. The "Our Target" row shows our property's target rents, and the rents at other properties:

Rent Comparables					
Apt Name	# Units	Year Built	Occupancy	Avg Rent	Avg $/SF
The Louis Overland Park	**293**	**1999**	**97%**	**1,962**	**1.49**
Bradford Pointe	306	1997	95%	1,855	1.63
Pointe Royal	437	1987	95%	1,452	1.62
Hunter's Pointe TH	333	1986	95%	1,420	1.52
Jefferson Pointe	390	2001	95%	1,697	1.48
Sandstone Creek	364	2001/2014	91%	1,470	1.43
Savoy Apartments	254	2001	90%	2,175	1.33
Corbin Crossing	298	2006	94%	1,780	1.66
Village at Lionsgate	360	2000	92%	1,625	1.52
The Ranch at Prairie Trace	280	2015	94%	1,493	1.62
Corbin Greens	228	2014	96%	1,622	1.65
Weston Point	350	1999	92%	1,494	1.54

Figure 65: The Louis Apartments Rent Comparables

We projected reducing vacancy to 5 percent and achieving our target rents in year three:

Turnover and Vacancy Assumptions			
	Year 1	Year 2	Year 3-5
Vacancy	10%	5%	5%
Bad Debt	1%	1%	1%
Loss to Lease	18%	12%	1%
Total	**29%**	**18%**	**7%**

Figure 66: The Louis Apartments Turnover and Vacancy Assumptions

And we projected selling the property in year five at a cap rate of 5.25 percent:

Sale	
Sale Year	5
Stabilized Cap Rate	5.25%
Sale Price	70,643,191
Loan Principal	(37,871,915)
Transaction Costs	(1,766,080)
Net Proceeds	**31,005,196**

Figure 67: The Louis Apartments Sale Assumptions

THE BIG PICTURE: DOES IT PASS THE SNIFF TEST?

You may not be an expert, but don't dismiss your gut intuition! Here are some questions to ask yourself:

1. Do you think the plan is achievable?
2. Do the timelines look realistic?
3. Do they have the team to execute the plan?

Looking back over our example ... what do you think? Achievable? Unrealistic? Risky?

> You may not be an expert, but don't dismiss your gut intuition.

Other Key Things to Look For

Back-loaded Returns. How much of the return is derived from cash flow vs. appreciation? Back-loaded returns come from appreciation, and appreciation is highly dependent on macroeconomic factors beyond operator control. That adds risk. Remember our exercise earlier in the chapter evaluating IRR and how the timing of payouts can impact the result? It is important to understand where most of the investor return will come from. If it's from cash flow, that significantly reduces the overall risk. If it's a combination, it's important to break it down between the two.

Look at figure 63. Notice cash flow averages $1.3 million per year, while the exit proceeds are $31 million. Clearly, this project's returns are mostly dependent on appreciation rather than cash flow. That makes it riskier than a "core" fully stabilized investment where the bulk of the returns come from cash flow. We projected a 17 percent IRR and a 22.5 percent ARR for our project, which is in line with risk.

Development investments are even more back-loaded and subject to other risks like cost and time overruns. Because of these added dimensions of risk, you should demand higher returns. I personally want to see returns of at least 20 percent for development projects.

The Income Test. As mentioned in chapter 17, debt is a key component of a successful investment—but also increases risk, especially at higher levels. You want debt in the "Goldilocks Zone"—not too much, and not too little. Deals go really bad when they cannot make their debt payments. From the capital stack exercise above you can tell why: The priority lenders can take over your deal, and it is possible for equity investors to have 100 percent losses.

But even the worst economic storms can be weathered as long as the debt can be paid. Values may crash and crises may come, but as long as you can pay the debt, you can hold on until the storm passes.

So you want to look at the cash flow versus the debt payments: How much risk is there that the debt can't be paid? It's important to understand the runway that the business plan predicts until the project is cash-flow positive. Will it take three months or three years? Investors may be surprised to find that many business plans will initially be cash-flow negative for a time. This is generally contemplated at the outset, but understanding the gap in cash flow and the time it takes to achieve breakeven is a key component to understanding the risk involved.

Sale	
Sale Year	5
Stabilized Cap Rate	5.25%
Sale Price	70,643,191
Loan Principal	(37,871,915)
Transaction Costs	(1,766,080)
Net Proceeds	31,005,196

Sale	
Sale Year	5
Stabilized Cap Rate	5.75%
Sale Price	64,500,305
Loan Principal	(37,871,915)
Transaction Costs	(1,766,080)
Net Proceeds	24,862,310

Sale	
Sale Year	5
Stabilized Cap Rate	6.25%
Sale Price	59,340,281
Loan Principal	(37,871,915)
Transaction Costs	(1,766,080)
Net Proceeds	19,702,285

Sale	
Sale Year	5
Stabilized Cap Rate	6.75%
Sale Price	54,944,704
Loan Principal	(37,871,915)
Transaction Costs	(1,766,080)
Net Proceeds	15,306,709

Figure 68: Northpark Example Cap Rate Sensitivity Analysis

Look again at figure 63. Notice the Debt Service Coverage Ratio (DSCR). Year one is 1.62x and climbs to 2.66x in year three. This means income is 162–266 percent of debt service—exceptionally strong. Banks typically want to see 1.25x or better, and this property delivers safely.

The Value Test. The second risk of leverage is that the value of the deal drops below the debt—getting "underwater." This is less important than the income test above, because as long as the debt is being paid, lenders generally will not act to take over a project. But you still want to look at possible scenarios where the value of the deal could drop below the value of the debt, because it means no exit is profitable.

Since we generated the majority of returns expected by this project at exit, it also makes sense to stress these assumptions. We projected a 5.25 percent cap rate exit, but what if it was higher? These tables show the results for four different exit cap rates.

At a 6.75 percent cap rate, we would still make money, albeit not much ($15.3 million sale proceeds on our $14.5 million investment).

This project passes the risk/reward test for me. Even if cap rates go up dramatically, I may not make much, but I won't lose anything. Remember, minimizing losses is far more important than maximizing gains. I think it is very unlikely that cap rates rise that high within five years. My conclusion is that I think the upside is realistic and probable, and in a worst-case scenario, I won't lose money. That's a winning formula!

> **WINNING FORMULA**
> The upside is probable, and the worst case is breakeven.

Cash Reserves. Another area to pay attention to is the adequacy of cash reserves. This is highly important in any deal that has negative cash flow or growth expenditures. If timelines or budgets are exceeded, the business will run out of cash (this is not uncommon). Then what? Someone will have to put more cash in. The sponsor will probably look to existing investors, and failing that, will be forced to liquidate the property, perhaps unfavorably. So why doesn't every deal have millions of cash in reserves? Because excess cash can dilute returns to investors. Sponsors generally don't like too much in reserves as it can drag down total return. However, in my opinion, it's always better to take a slightly lower return and have ample cash reserves.

In our example, cash reserves are $200,000 in working capital and $600,000 in interest reserves (figure 63). Digging a little deeper, I found a 5 percent contingency on construction costs. That seems ample to me, especially given that it was projected to cash flow right away.

Other Risks. You have to decide what you think. How could this project go bad? Let's think of some ways:

- Renovations aren't completed on time. But since the property is already cash-flowing strongly, delays might extend the exit timeline but not put the property at risk.
- A property manager drops the ball and doesn't increase the rents by year three. Again, because of strong cash flow, this would just cause delays but not put it at risk.
- It requires refinance in year three because the senior debt matures, making this project highly dependent on the credit markets. Will lending be available? At what rates? They projected they could refinance at a 6 percent interest rate, a 6 percent cap rate, and 65 percent LTV.
- Those are all fairly conservative, but it would be wise to stress-test them. Using the spreadsheet provided, I put in 7 percent interest rate, 6.25 percent cap rate, and 60 percent LTV to see what would happen. It fell short of being able to pay off the preferred equity by $227,000. Even in this extreme scenario, the refi was almost possible. To me, this was acceptable, but also demonstrated the risks.

See, you *can* understand the numbers with just a modest investment of time. And the more you do it, the more familiar you will get and the quicker you will become.

Once you have done your initial review, schedule a call with your sponsor to go over it and ask questions!

CONCLUSION

Throughout this book, we've explored the powerful investment strategies that billionaires use to build and preserve wealth—focusing on private alternatives like private credit, private equity, venture capital, real assets, and other exclusive opportunities. By stepping beyond traditional stocks and bonds, you can unlock higher returns, greater stability, and access to wealth-building strategies that most investors never tap into.

Now, it's time to take action. Investing like a billionaire isn't just for the ultrawealthy—it's a mindset and a strategy that anyone can adopt. You don't have to do it all at once, but as you begin incorporating private alts into your portfolio, you'll be glad you did.

Over time, these strategies can help you multiply wealth faster and with less risk, just as the most successful investors do. Remember that every billionaire started somewhere, and you have the tools to follow in their footsteps. Keep learning, stay disciplined, and focus on the long game—because that's how real wealth is built.

Well, at this point, you are ready for your journey following in billionaires' investment footsteps. To keep you inspired and resourced on your private alts path, subscribe to the *Invest Like a Billionaire* podcast and take advantage of our billionaire investor ecosystem at investlikeabillionaire.org. Thank you for taking this journey with us—we can't wait to see where your investing success takes you!

CONCLUSION

APPENDIX A

IF YOU'RE NOT ACCREDITED

*All I ask is the chance to prove
that money can't make me happy.*
— **Spike Milligan**

Most of this book is specifically written for accredited investors. But what if you are not accredited? Most investors started unaccredited, of course, and in this appendix, we will cover what you can do to get started as an unaccredited investor.

SECURITIES LAW

First off, here is a very incomplete thumbnail sketch of US securities law. "Securities" are defined by three characteristics:

1. The expectation of profits.
2. A common enterprise.
3. Depending solely on the efforts of others for success.

Thus, most passive investments are classified as securities, which creates the issue. Securities are highly regulated in order to protect investors from shady enterprises. To be sold to the public, a security must be *registered* with the SEC. Registration is a very involved, very expensive process that basically makes you a public company, like the companies that are listed on stock exchanges.

The alternative to registration is to find an *exemption* from registration. There are two exemptions that are commonly used: Reg D 506(b) and 506(c).

506(b) allows up to thirty-five nonaccredited investors to invest, so long as they have a substantial preexisting relationship with the sponsor. This exemption specifically prohibits "general solicitation"—e.g., marketing, advertising, or even a web page.

506(c) allows unlimited accredited investors, and their accreditation status must be verified. General solicitation is permitted.

GO ACTIVE

The best and most common way for nonaccredited investors to invest is to *go active*. The third requirement of a security (above) is that it "depends solely on the efforts of others for its success." Thus, if you are actively managing the investment, it is not a security, and it is legal for you to invest.

> **The best and most common way for nonaccredited investors to invest is to go active.**

Should You Go Active? Many years ago, I tried my hand at personal real estate ownership and bought a duplex. As it turns out, I am just not cut out for hands-on real estate management as a side gig. I had too many repairs, budget-breaking remodels, multiple deadbeat tenants, evictions, lots of property damage, and midnight phone calls. I finally hired a property manager. Things started getting better, but I still could never achieve the profits my spreadsheet promised. I sold it at a loss and practically danced for joy.

On the other hand, my daughter bought a house and rented it out (despite my dire warnings!) and had no issues. She pocketed a handsome income monthly and had even more appreciation.

Why was she successful when I wasn't? I had a demanding job with lots of travel, and the rental was a distant afterthought. *I treated it as if it were passive when it wasn't.* I never had the time or energy or desire to learn how to be a great landlord.

> **If you have a demanding job and/or family life, or you are not excited about rolling up your sleeves and getting your hands dirty, don't go active.**

If you have a demanding job and/or family life, or you are not excited about rolling up your sleeves and getting your hands dirty, *don't go active*.

If you want to go active, here are some of the most popular:

Residential Fix and Flip. The learning curve can be steep especially if you do not have a lot of history in the trades. But a lot of folks buy beat-up properties, fix them, and sell or rent them. It's way beyond the scope of this book to tell you how to do it, but resources are not hard to find.

Short-Term Rentals. Buying or renting a house and listing it on sites like Airbnb can be very lucrative. Make no mistake though, you are in the hospitality business, and a lot of hustle is required. Again, way beyond our scope here, but there are lots of support resources online.

Long-Term Rentals and Medium-Term Rentals. These are other options you can explore that have some advantages (less work) and some drawbacks (lower profits).

Joint Ventures. If you have some folks you want to partner with to share the work, you can partner with them in a member-managed LLC.

To be active, you must do more than just supply capital. Presumably you and your partners can divvy up the work so that each is doing what they are good at.

Here is an example. Maybe you have a demanding job, but you are good with numbers. You have a hardworking, trusted friend who is eager to do the day-to-day work. You decide how to share the responsibilities, who will make what decisions, and how you will split the costs and profits. You write that all up into an LLC operating agreement.

REG A+

Added in 2012, the Reg A+ is in essence a "light" version of an SEC registration. It takes much less cost and effort (though still significant) and allows the sponsor to sell shares to the public, with limitations. Most Reg A+ offerings are investments into operating businesses with the associated high risk. There are fewer real estate deals, but I have seen some offerings I like. An online search should give you some options. Follow the recommendations in this book, the same as any private offering.

506(B)

This exemption is the one historically used by sponsors. But recall the regulations above: Sponsors are not allowed to advertise. This means you must know the sponsor already.

There are a couple of options to approach this.

The first is to find a sponsor you like and get to know them and ask about 506(b) offerings they might have. Our firm, Aspen Funds, tries to do one 506(b) offering per year as a service to nonaccredited investors. This takes some extra time and effort for sponsors. We first offer an unannounced 506(b) and open it up to our existing unaccredited relationships. Then we close that offering and do a 506(c) as normal.

The other approach is to find and hire a financial advisor who offers 506(b) private alternatives. But as we have discussed, very few understand alts, know where to get them, and will recommend them (see chapter 3). The alts they can access are usually offered by broker-dealers and are fee-laden—see "How to Spot the Losers" (chapter 17) and "Navigate a PPM In Thirty Minutes" (chapter 18).

BECOME A GP

There are more ways than one to *go active*. One way is to form your own fund and be the General Partner (GP). For example, you can form a member-managed LLC and become the manager, raise funds from Limited Partners (LPs), and buy and manage a property. Because you are active, you can (and should) invest your own funds.

Most do this under the 506(b) exemption and approach friends and family. You should consult an attorney for the dos and don'ts—but *do not* build a website, post the offer on social media, or email or call people you don't have a relationship with!

Another way to become a GP and offer more sophisticated institutional class investments to your investors is through a *fund-of-funds*. Here's how it works: You find a sponsor you like and offer to invest as a fund in their offering. You form your own fund as a GP *to invest (as an LP) in your sponsor's offering*. You make your own PPM, do your own tax return, send your own reports, etc. Some sponsors, including my own, have a fund-of-funds program. In our case, we offer more favorable returns (so you can earn income), and we support our fund-of-funds investors with back-office support to simplify your efforts.

If your sponsor's offering is a 506(c), yours will be as well. You can make a web page, post on social media, etc. You are required to verify that your investors are accredited. Your fund is accredited by virtue of the fact that all of its members are accredited. If your sponsor's offering is a 506(b), yours will be too. You can only approach people you have a preexisting relationship with, and you can raise from up to thirty-five nonaccredited investors.

BECOMING AN RIA

The final approach may surprise you. Become a Registered Investment Advisor (RIA): an individual who is licensed to offer investment advice to clients.

As an RIA you are automatically accredited. (In 2020, the SEC expanded the definition of accredited investors to include RIAs.) Becoming a licensed RIA does not mean you actually have to advise investors—it just means you are licensed to do so.

And it's surprisingly easy if you have the mind for it.

You'll have to pass the Series 65 Exam. Years ago, I got the study materials and dove in. It took me about a month part-time to know the ins and outs. If you pass the exam, there are just a few more steps to becoming a licensed RIA:

1. Create an LLC for your RIA firm.
2. Because you will presumably manage less than $25 million in assets, you will have to register your firm with your state's financial regulator.
3. An exemption to #2 above is "only to an adviser that provides investment advice to clients exclusively through an "interactive website." In other words, a web page that dispenses investment advice.[77]
4. Next, go to the SEC's IARD website and file a form ADV.
5. Finally, go to the FINRA site and file a U-4.

Yes, this is a bit involved, but it's certainly doable for the highly committed. A helpful blog on Achievable.com documented the process,[78] but you should get a securities attorney to help you.

APPENDIX B

FAT TAILS

Most investors are familiar with the concept of volatility. What few understand, however, is the risk posed by the concept of *fat tails*. This is perhaps the most critical thing you should know about the public markets that billionaires and some academics know, but few others do.

Before I describe fat tails, I will share a story about the terrible price of ignoring them.

In 1997, another Nobel Prize was awarded, this time to Myron Scholes for his work on the groundbreaking 1973 Black-Scholes model for the pricing of financial derivatives.

In 1994, Myron Scholes and Robert Merton came together with John Meriwether to found Long Term Capital Management (LTCM), a hedge fund based on their mathematical models. They quickly raised $1 billion from business owners, celebrities, university endowments, and the Italian central bank. Confident in their mathematics, they leveraged up 25 to 1, then 150 to 1, controlling derivatives with $1.25 trillion in notional value. Their first year, they returned 21 percent; the next, 43 percent; and 41 percent in their third. Their genius, their mathematical secret sauce, and their incredible returns were unmatched, and they became the envy of Wall Street.

Then, in 1998, they were hit by the Russian financial crisis, when the Russian government defaulted on its domestic bonds. In a remarkable five-week period in September 1998, LTCM's equity tumbled from $2.3 billion to essentially zero. Their financial footprint was so large, experts began to fear that the global financial system was at risk. The Federal

Reserve Bank of New York organized an emergency $3.625 billion private bailout. The saga has been well told in one of my favorite books, *When Genius Failed: The Rise and Fall of Long-Term Capital Management*, by Roger Lowenstein.

The spectacular failure of LTCM is a graphic example of the failure of mathematical models when applied to the markets. Financial models can be accurate most of the time, but they have a fatal flaw: *They underrepresent the risk of extreme events.*

All financial modeling is based on a branch of mathematics called *statistics*, which measures the probabilities related to random variables: things like SAT scores, baseball batting averages, or the amount of lint in a person's pocket. Random variables fall into something called a *normal distribution* pattern, or *bell curve*.

The problem is this: The markets *do not behave like random variables* and *do not follow a normal distribution pattern*.

Over short time periods, markets do in fact mimic random data. In figure 10, the left chart shows the market movements of the S&P 500 (the circles) for a single year (2023) compared to a normal distribution (the dotted line). You can see the market movements track precisely, and with a 99.5 percent correlation.

But over a longer period of time, the problem becomes apparent. The market is subject to more extreme moves much more often than is statistically predicted.[79] The chart on the right shows that over longer time periods, the market diverges materially from a normal distribution at the extremes. Notice how far the plot deviates from the dotted line, which, again, is what would be expected if the data behaved randomly.

A prime example is Black Monday, October 19, 1987, when the S&P 500 fell 20 percent in a single day. Mathematically, this was a "25-sigma event"—25 standard deviations from normal. To put that in context, an 8-sigma event would happen only once since the dawn of the universe 13.7 billion years ago.[80] A 25-sigma event is less likely than a tornado ripping

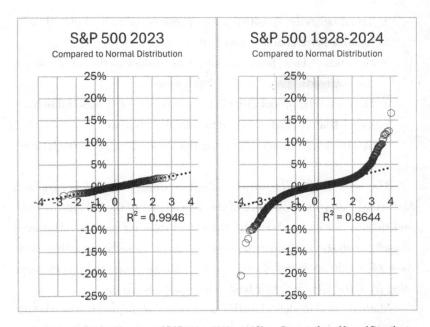

Figure 10: Market Movement of S&P 500 in 2023 vs. 96 Years Compared to a Normal Distribution

through a junkyard and leaving behind a completed 747. What a 25-sigma event *really* means is that your math is flawed.

Actual market movement *appears* random, especially when viewed over short time periods, which allows mathematical formulas to be applied with great accuracy. However, over longer periods, the markets exhibit extreme behavior both more commonly and more extremely than random variables do—a phenomenon called *kurtosis*, or more commonly, "fat tails." This was the miscalculation of LTCM.

Data shows the stock market does not move randomly, but has many distinctive characteristics when compared to random variables—and as a professional trader for many years, I can personally attest to all of these:[81]

▸ Volatility clustering—large price changes tend to be followed by large price changes, and small price changes tend to be followed by small price changes.

- Trend behavior—positive price changes tend to be followed by positive price changes, and vice versa.
- Skewness—large price changes tend to skew to the upside or the downside.
- Fat tails—the probability of extreme profits or losses is much larger than predicted by the normal distribution.
- Tail thickness temporality—tail thickness changes through time.

The issue is that *statistical methods only apply to random variables*. Mathematicians are well aware of the deficiencies of the existing models, and debate continues about the validity of existing models.[82] However, financial analysts continue to apply statistical methods because they work most of the time—rarely if ever pointing out the potential errors stemming from the fact that their basic assumption is wrong.

Mathematical models like MPT are indeed helpful and produce better portfolios with better results. But they are also misleading because they vastly underrepresent downside tail risk.

ACKNOWLEDGMENTS

Special thanks to:
Terrance Wise for his research assistance in the real estate chapter, and for being a very cool dude.

Steve Woodruff for his inspiration in recognizing the importance of writing this book, and for his insights as an RIA.

Jim Dew for being a "unicorn" financial advisor and also for helping with this book.

NOTES

Chapter 2: What Makes Billionaires Different from You and Me

1. Carrie McCabe, "Asset Managers Ready for Retail $3 Trillion Into Alternatives," *Forbes*, February 1, 2023, https://www.forbes.com/sites/carriemccabe/2023/02/01/asset-managers-ready-for-retail-3-trillion-into-alternatives/.
2. Yaël Bizouati-Kennedy, "How Kevin O'Leary Grows Wealth: 'I Think of my Money as Soldiers'," GOBankingRates, October 6, 2023, https://www.nasdaq.com/articles/how-kevin-oleary-grows-wealth:-i-think-of-my-money-as-soldiers.

Chapter 3: 7 Things Your Financial Advisor Will Never Tell You

3. "Alternatives in 2022," Preqin, January 11, 2022, https://www.preqin.com/insights/research/reports/alternatives-in-2022.
4. Samantha Lamas, "Why Do Investors Hire Their Financial Advisor?" *Morningstar*, June 16, 2023, https://www.morningstar.com/financial-advice/why-do-investors-hire-their-financial-advisor.

Chapter 4: What Billionaires Know About the Stock Market

5. Kevin Dowd et al., "How Unlucky is 25-Signa?" March 24, 2008, https://arxiv.org/ftp/arxiv/papers/1103/1103.5672.pdf.
6. "The Correlation Conundrum," Swan Global Investments (2022), https://www.swanglobalinvestments.com/the-correlation-conundrum/.
7. "Why We Have a Correlation Bubble," J.P. Morgan, October 5, 2010, https://www.newconstructs.com/wp-content/uploads/2010/10/JP-Morgan-and-Correlation.
8. Michael Dunleavy, CFA, "Overestimating Liquidity Needs Can Undercut the Return Potential of US Pension Plans," *Cambridge Asso-*

ciates, (blog), November 2021, https://www.cambridgeassociates.com/en-eu/insight/overestimating-liquidity-needs-can-undercut-the-return-potential-of-us-pension-plans/.
9   "What is George Soros' Game?" Graham Value, https://www.graham-value.com/blog/what-george-soros-game.
10 James K. Glassman, "Trusting Markets to Be Efficient," *Washington Post*, June 14, 2003, https://www.washingtonpost.com/archive/business/2003/06/15/trusting-markets-to-be-efficient/66e3f564-0e91-419e-b71b-a530161aca5b/.
11 Karl Kaufman, "'The Market Is Always Wrong': In Defense of Inefficiency," *Forbes*, September 30 2018, https://www.forbes.com/sites/karlkaufman/2018/09/30/the-market-is-always-wrong-in-defense-of-inefficiency/.
12 "Efficient Markets," MastersInvest.com, https://mastersinvest.com/efficientmarketsquotes#:-:text=%E2%80%9CNaturally%20the%20disservice%20done%20students,Frank%20Martin.
13 *The Big Short*, dir. Adam McKay, Regency Enterprises, 2015.
14 Markus K. Brunnermeier, Stefan Nagel, "Arbitrage at Its Limits: Hedge Funds and the Technology Bubble," May/October 2002, PDF, http://www.econ.yale.edu/-shiller/behfin/2002-04-11/brunnermeier-nagel.pdf.
15 Mattia C., "The Man Who Bet Against the DotCom Bubble, and Missed It by a Whisker," *Medium*, (blog), January 23, 2019, https://medium.com/@mattia-c/the-man-who-bet-against-the-dotcom-bubble-and-missed-it-by-a-whisker-76d8da367d55.
16 Janes A. Dorn, "Reflections on Greenspan's 'Irrational Exuberance' Speech After 25 Years," Cato Institute, December 27, 2001, https://www.cato.org/blog/reflections-greenspans-irrational-exuberance-speech-after-25-years.
17 Amazon.com, Inc. (AMZN), Historical Prices table, Yahoo! Finance, https://finance.yahoo.com/quote/AMZN/history/?period1=863703000&period2=1742306800.
18 Ibid.
19 *2001 Annual Report*, Amazon.com, January 24, 2002, https://s2.q4cdn.com/299287126/files/doc_financials/annual/2001annualreport.pdf.
20 David Swensen, *Unconventional Success: A Fundamental Approach to*

Personal Investment (Simon & Schuster, 2005), 159–161.
21. Brian Knowles, "Looking in the Wrong Places for Returns: Four Common Mistakes," BlackRock, https://www.blackrock.com/institutions/en-axj/insights/four-investment-mistakes.
22. *Behavior Patterns and Pitfalls of U.S. Investors,* Federal Research Division, Library of Congress, in agreement with the Securities and Exchange Commission, August 2010, https://www.sec.gov/investor/locinvestorbehaviorreport.pdf.
23. Ibid., 11.
24. Ibid., 13.
25. Ibid., 8.
26. Nassim Taleb, *Fooled by Randomness: The Hidden Role of Chance in Life and in the Markets* (Random House, 2008).
27. Jeannine Mancini, "Charlie Munger Warned: '95% of People Have No Chance of Beating S&P 500 Index—but Adds 'Why Shouldn't Life Be Hard?'" *Yahoo! Finance*, August 22, 2024, https://finance.yahoo.com/news/charlie-munger-warned-95-people-151518884.html.

Chapter 5: What Makes Private Alts So Attractive

28. Hayden Gallary, "Better Alternative(s): Private Investments May Improve Outcomes for Defined Contribution Plan Participants," Cambridge Associates, March 8, 2024, https://www.cambridgeassociates.com/wp-content/uploads/2024/03/2024-03-Better-Alternatives-PI-May-Improve-Outcomes-for-DC-Plan-Participants.pdf.
29. "Guide to Alternatives," 4Q 2024, as of November 30, 2024, J.P. Morgan, https://am.jpmorgan.com/us/en/asset-management/institutional/insights/market-insights/guide-to-alternatives/.
30. Ibid.
31. Rebecca Burns, "Public Pensions Invest Big in BlackStone's Controversial Rental Properties," *Aljazeera America*, October 16, 2015, https://www.tenantstogether.org/updates/public-pensions-invest-big-blackstones-controversial-rental-properties.
32. Portfolio for the Future, CAIA Association (2022), https://caia.org/portfolio-for-the-future.
33. Andrew Bary, "Crash Course," *Barron's*, November 10, 2008, https://

www.barrons.com/articles/SB122610188023510005.
34. David Swensen, guest lecture, Yale University, Econ 252: Financial Markets (Robert Schiller), April 9, 2020, https://bookdown.org/Albert/finance-shiller/guest-speaker-david-swensen.html; https://oyc.yale.edu/economics/econ-252.
35. Ibid.
36. Jason Zweig, "Yale Invests This Way. Should You?" *Wall Street Journal*, March 10, 2023, https://www.wsj.com/articles/yale-university-endowment-alternative-assets-b4bd3258.
37. Richard M. Ennis, "The Fairy Tale of Alternative Investing," (blog), March 17, 2022, https://richardmennis.com/blog/the-fairy-tale-of-alternative-investing.
38. "Yale Reports Investment Return for Fiscal 2024," YaleNews, October 25, 2024, https://news.yale.edu/2024/10/25/yale-reports-investment-return-fiscal-2024.

Chapter 6: Private Real Estate

39. J.P. Morgan, "Guide to Alternatives," https://am.jpmorgan.com/us/en/asset-management/adv/insights/market-insights/guide-to-alternatives/.
40. Ibid.
41. Josh Lerner, "Yale University Investments Office: February 2015," Harvard Business School, April 2015, https://www.hbs.edu/faculty/Pages/item.aspx?num=49035.

Chapter 8: Private Equity

42. Nicolas Rabener, "Private Equity: Fooling Some of the People All of the Time?" CFA Institute, Enterprising In-vestor, January 20, 2020, https://blogs.cfainstitute.org/investor/2020/01/20/private-equity-fooling-some-of-the-people-all-of-the-time.
43. David Swensen, *Unconventional Success: A Fundamental Approach to Personal Investment* (Simon & Schuster; 2005), 134.
44. Ibid., 136.

Chapter 9: Venture Capital
45 David Swensen, *Unconventional Success: A Fundamental Approach to Personal Investment* (Simon & Schuster, 2005), 139.
46 David Swensen, guest lecture, Yale University, Econ 252: Financial Markets (Robert Schiller), April 9, 2020, https://bookdown.org/Albert/finance-shiller/guest-speaker-david-swensen.html; https://oyc.yale.edu/economics/econ-252.

Chapter 10: Hedge Funds
47 David Swensen, *Unconventional Success: A Fundamental Approach to Personal Investment* (Simon & Schuster, 2005), 132.

Chapter 11: Oil & Gas, Gold, Crypto, and More
48 *Net Zero Roadmap: A Global Pathway to Keep the 1.5°C Goal in Reach*, International Energy Agency (September 2023), Executive Summary, https://www.iea.org/reports/net-zero-roadmap-a-global-pathway-to-keep-the-15-0c-goal-in-reach/executive-summary.
49 Josh Lerner, "Yale University Investments Office: February 2015," Harvard Business School, April 2015, https://www.hbs.edu/faculty/Pages/item.aspx?num=49035.
50 Ibid.
51 Ibid.
52 Nick Lioudis, "What Is the Gold Standard? History and Collapse," Investopedia, updated October 14, 2024, https://www.investopedia.com/ask/answers/09/gold-standard.asp.
53 Adam Hayes, "What Happens to Bitcoin After All 21 Million Are Mined?" Investopedia, December 22, 2024, https://www.investopedia.com/tech/what-happens-bitcoin-after-21-million-mined/.
54 "How Bitcoin Can Scale," *River Learn*, (blog), https://river.com/learn/how-bitcoin-can-scale/.
55 Angus Berwick and Ben Foldy, "The Shadow Dollar That's Fueling the Financial Underworld," *Wall Street Journal*, September 10, 2024, https://www.wsj.com/finance/currencies/tether-crypto-us-dollar-sanctions-52f85459.

Chapter 12: Stocks and Bonds

56 Amy C. Arnott, "Why Fund Returns Are Lower Than You Might Think," Morningstar, August 30, 2021, https://www.morningstar.com/funds/why-fund-returns-are-lower-than-you-might-think.

57 Josh Lerner, "Yale University Investments Office: February 2015," Harvard Business School, April 2015, https://www.hbs.edu/faculty/Pages/item.aspx?num=49035.

58 Ibid.

59 Ibid.

60 Ibid.

61 Ibid., 27.

Chapter 13: How Billionaires Beat the Tax Man

62 Jesse Eisenger et al., "The Secret IRS Files: Trove of Never-Before-Seen Records Reveal How the Wealthiest Avoid Income Tax," ProPublica, June 8, 2021, https://www.propublica.org/article/the-secret-irs-files-trove-of-never-before-seen-records-reveal-how-the-wealthiest-avoid-income-tax.

63 "Publication 925: Passive Activity and At-Risk Rules" (2024), IRS, http://www.irs.gov/pub/irs-pdf/p925.pdf.

Chapter 14: Organizing and Structuring Your Investments

64 Sheryl Nance-Nash, "Can You Deduct Your Vacation from Your Taxes?" *Afar*, January 31, 2024, https://www.afar.com/magazine/how-to-legally-write-off-your-vacation.

65 Ibid.

66 Ibid.

Chapter 15: Building a Smart Portfolio

67 David Swensen, guest lecture, Yale University, Econ 252: Financial Markets (Robert Schiller), April 9, 2020, https://bookdown.org/Albert/finance-shiller/guest-speaker-david-swensen.html; https://oyc.yale.edu/economics/econ-252.

68 Sarah Min, "Warren Buffett's Berkshire Hathaway Has Been a Fortress Stock During Recessions and Bear Markets. Here's How,"

CNBC, May 5, 2023, https://www.cnbc.com/2023/05/05/warren-buffetts-berkshire-hathaway-has-been-a-fortress-stock-during-recessions-and-bear-markets-heres-how.html.
69 Lerner, "Yale University Investments Office."
70 Ibid.
71 David Swensen, guest lecture, Yale University, Econ 252: Financial Markets (Robert Schiller), April 9, 2020, https://bookdown.org/Albert/finance-shiller/guest-speaker-david-swensen.html; https://oyc.yale.edu/economics/econ-252.

Chapter 16: How to Select an Operator
72 "What Makes Warren Buffett a Great Investor? Intelligence of Discipline?" *Farnam Street Media*, (blog), https://fs.blog/what-makes-warren-buffett-a-great-investor/.
73 David Swensen, *Unconventional Success: A Fundamental Approach to Personal Investment* (Simon & Schuster, 2005), 144.
74 Ibid.

Chapter 17: How to Spot the Losers
75 Ponzitracker: The Ponzi Scheme Authority, https://www.ponzitracker.com/.
76 Swensen, *Unconventional Success*, 70.

Appendix A: If You're Not Accredited
77 "Exemption for Certain Investment Advisers Operating Through the Internet," Federal Register, US National Archives and Records Administration, https://www.federalregister.gov/documents/2002/12/18/02-31843/exemption-for-certain-investment-advisers-operating-through-the-internet.
78 Tyler York, "How to Become an Accredited Investor," *Achievable*, (blog), June 17, 2022, https://blog.achievable.me/careers-in-finance/how-to-become-an-accredited-investor/.

Appendix B: Fat Tails

79 Sudhalahari Bommareddy et al., "Applications of Fat Tail Models in Financial Markets," George Mason University, Spring 2014, https://www3.gmu.edu/schools/vse/seor/studentprojects/graduate/2014Spring/FinancialEngineering/Report.pdf.

80 Kevin Dowd et al., "How Unlucky is 25-Sigma?" March 24, 2008, https://arxiv.org/ftp/arxiv/papers/1103/1103.5672.pdf.

81 Stoyan V. Stoyanov et al., "Fat-Tailed Models for Risk Estimation," Karlsruher Institut für Technologie, May 2011, https://www.econstor.eu/obitstream/10419/45631/1/659400324.pdf.

82 Ibid.

ABOUT THE AUTHORS

 Bob Fraser is CFO and chief macro strategist for Aspen Funds, a fund sponsor in multiple asset classes, including private credit, commercial real estate, distressed debt, energy, and others. Aspen focuses on data-driven investing, identifying top macro trends, and constructing opportunistic investment funds. Bob is known for his data-driven and paradigm-shifting lectures, and is co-host of Aspen's *Invest Like a Billionaire* podcast. He is a former *magna cum laude* UC Berkeley computer scientist, tech startup founder, and Ernst & Young Entrepreneur of the Year Award winner. Bob has been happily married for forty years and has four amazing grown children.

 Ben Fraser is CIO and managing director of Aspen Funds and is responsible for sourcing, vetting, and capital formation of investments. Ben has experience as a commercial banker and underwriter, as well as in boutique asset management. A contributor on the Forbes Finance Council, he is also a co-host of the *Invest Like a Billionaire* podcast. Ben completed his MBA at Azusa Pacific University, and his BS in finance from the University of Kansas, graduating *magna cum laude*.

INVEST LIKE A BILLIONAIRE PODCAST

Most investors don't know that the ultrawealthy (billionaires, institutions, family offices) have large portions of their investment portfolios allocated to investments outside the stock market and in alternatives like real estate, private equity, and hedge funds. Meanwhile, the average high-net-worth investor is mostly invested in stocks and bonds.

Join Bob Fraser, Jim Maffuccio, and Ben Fraser on the *Invest Like a Billionaire* podcast as they dive into the world of alternative investments, uncover strategies of the ultrawealthy, discuss economics, and interview successful investors and alternative investment experts.

ABOUT ASPEN FUNDS

Aspen Funds (www.aspenfunds.us) is a boutique private investment manager. Aspen specializes in identifying key macro trends and developing private investments for high-net-worth individuals and institutions to capitalize on them. Some of our sectors have included distressed debt, private credit, upstream oil and gas, and multiple classes of real estate: multifamily, industrial, retail and self-storage. Aspen has been on the *Inc. 5000* list of fastest-growing companies for several years.